Davey's Half-Way Home Cafe

Davey Doby

authorHOUSE®

AuthorHouse™
1663 Liberty Drive
Bloomington, IN 47403
www.authorhouse.com
Phone: 1-800-839-8640

First published by AuthorHouse   07/01/2011

ISBN: 978-1-4567-2669-0 (sc)
ISBN: 978-1-4567-2671-3 (dj)
ISBN: 978-1-4567-2670-6 (ebk)

Library of Congress Control Number: 2011901224

Printed in the United States of America

About the Author

My name is Francis Earline Edison and I was born on December 4, 1929. I was the eighth child, third daughter, born to Edd and Lela Edison. I have been trying to cook as long as I can remember. My mama taught me to do my best, even if it was only field peas, corn bread, and Kool aid. Now after 70 years, I want to leave my soul food recipes to my sons and all of my customers at

Davey's Half Way Home Cafe
5628 Hwy. 15
Louin, MS 39338
Community of Montrose, MS

I love all of you.
These recipes were written for small restaurants.

Acknowledgement of the Author

Earline Broomfield is an icon in south Mississippi where she was raised. Known around the United States and the free world as the "Queen of Home-style," she has gained popularity and notoriety for her home-style recipes. One only had to visit her son's name-sake café, Davey's Half Way Home, to see how her iconic way of preparing and serving her cuisine would turn into an unforgettable dining experience. The uniqueness of everything she ever did in the field of culinary arts was broadcast far and wide by those who experienced it.

Prior to her retirement in May 2010 at the ripe "young" age of 80, Miss Earline, as she was known to everyone, would work in her kitchen "chopping" t-bones and rib-eyes with her spatula until they "wuz jes rite." I will never forget that cling, cling, click, click sound of her tenderizing those plate size steaks as they simmered on the grill. I will never forget the card tables that served as her buffet being loaded down with coleslaw garnished with raisins, fried pig skins, stuffed eggs, potato salad and the little styrofoam bowls to put all them in.

Then there were the pies and cakes she kept in a pie cabinet with a screen door; the coconut cake, the Glenn Parker cake, the Elvis Presley cake, the chocolate cake and an ever ending assortment of chocolate, lemon, coconut, pecan, tater and pumpkin pies, banana pudding and other "fattening" stuff.

I remember driving up to Davey's Half Way Home Café one Friday night and finding it closed. My first thoughts were "something's happened to Miss Earline." We were right; she had retired the day before to the shock and awe of everyone. She had worn herself out. 25 years of unselfishness had taken its toll, the time had come to hang up her apron.

I'm sure she misses the hustle and bustle of the life she lived in the kitchen making others happy, but she will never know how much those of us who had the privilege of eating Miss Earline's cooking miss her. It just isn't the same without the matriarch of southern cooking doing her thing. There has never been, nor will there ever be, a personality to grace our lives as the likes of Miss Earline Broomfield. But perhaps these recipes will allow you to experience a little of what you missed.

Mr. Richard Headrick
President and CEO Headrick Companies

TABLE OF CONTENTS

SCRIPTURE CAKE

1 cup Judges 5:25	1/2 cup Judges 4:19
2 cups Jeremiah 6:20	4 1/2 cups 1st Kings 4:22
3 T 1st Samuel 14:25	2 T Amos 4:5
6 Jeremiah 17:11	1/2 cup 1st Samuel 30:12
1/2 cup 1st Samuel 30:12	1/2 cup Nehemiah 13:12

Cream Judges and Jeremiah together. Add 3 T 1st Samuel. Add Jeremiah one at a time, beating continually. With a large spoon stir in 1st Samuel, add 1/2 cup Judges, alternating with 1st Kings. Stir in Amos and 1st Samuel, mixing well. Pour in bundt pan that has been greased and floured. Cook at 350 degrees for 1 hour, 15 minutes. When done, pour 1/4 cup Nehemiah over cake. Wrap cake in cheese cloth. After 24 hours, pour other half of Nehemiah over cheese cloth and cake. (The following ingredients are found in the above scripture verses: butter, sugar, honey, eggs, figs, milk, flour, baking powder, raisins and I prefer grape wine)

Millie McGee

DAVEY'S RESTAURANT

Country Cookin'
at it's finest

THIS BOOK IS DEDICATED WITH LOVE TO MY SONS MELVIN SHIPP, ARTHUR AND DAVEY DOBY, AND MY PARENTS EDD AND LELA EDISON

EARLINE BROOMFIELD
CHILD NO. 8

I am writing this book from the suggestion of the many people who came into Davey's Restaurant and pretended this was the best food they had ever eaten.

To my surprise, collard greens was always the topic for discussion. People would say things like "What is your secret on cooking collard greens?"

SO HERE IS MY SECRET!

Pick 'um, wash 'um, cut 'um, put meat in 'um (bacon grease or lard), salt in 'um with fresh jalapeno pepper in 'um, cook 'um, serve 'um, and EAT 'UM.

My mama, who I believe was the best cook who ever passed through Mississippi, handed down this recipe. She never had a job except cooking for her family and cooking for what she called her tractor meeting, which is now called revival.

Good Hope Church was built six miles south of Hickory, Mississippi. This day has been a special day. First Sunday in August for many years, at least before I was born, a young bull (you call it a steer) was killed for fresh meat. The first sweet potatoes were scratched (dug) by Papa, so Mama could make her good sweet potato pie.

Ever since I can remember, I was excited about the cooking and was always trying to help. Your Uncle Ardell said Mama left the cooking to me when I was about 9 years old while she took the boys and went to the field to chop cotton or thin the corn. I know this is all Latin to you. So anything you do not understand, ask some one born before 1945 or soon after. Davey, before you and Arthur came on the scene, I had been taught how to take very little food and make a meal "fit for a king".

I cannot remember many times we ate without meat. Your grandfather always kept a hog in the pig pen ready to kill, especially in the winter time. My father would preserve the meat by packing it in a lot of salt (I call myself writing modern now by using the word 'preserve') such as the hams, front shoulder and middling, which you call the bacon. Meanwhile, Mama would cook the fresh backbone and ribs we canned in jars. Therefore we had fresh meat way over in March (all winter) which used to be the spring of the year. We even canned the sausage. I told you all this to let you know we always had meat, peas, bread and Kool Aid for dinner, that was at 12 o'clock noon. I had to cook enough for supper, which was when we came out of the fields - at sundown. Supper had no certain time. It is supper time when you finish milking the cows, feeding the horses, chickens, hogs and bringing in stove wood. We would bathe in the No. 3 tub before the water got cold (which had been set out in the sun to warm. "You did not know that did you, Davey!")

There is so much I would love to tell you about old times, but the most important old things for me are very new for you. These things will stand throughout eternity such as morals, self-respect and respect for other people. Be truthful and treat people like you want to be treated, give to people who need a helping hand, in other words: Read and do Exodus, 20th chapter, verses 12-17 and Matthew 22nd chapter, verse 37; and always remember "If Jesus can put money in a fish's mouth, He can put money in your pocket." To find these words you must read your bible a little further (it is in there). For me those were the good times, because I know my mother and father loved and protected us and taught us to love one another. About the Jolly Aid Kool Aid - Mama traded eggs for it if she did not have a nickel. We would meet the store truck over on the main road and buy a candy bar for a few pennies, which was so hard to come by. "Davey let me tell you about the ice. We were so glad to see the iceman coming!"

9

Papa or Mama would save that dime to give the iceman for a small block of ice and Mama would wrap it up in an old raggedy quilt, kept especially to wrap the ice. We had a hole dug in the ground filled with sawdust to keep the ice in so it would not melt so fast.

Now I will tell you about Fourth of July. It was a doozy (it was a ball). About this time we would almost be finished with chopping and hoeing the cotton and thinning the corn. Mama would get her molasses can and make it full of ice cream. Then we would put the can in a foot tub and put ice and salt around the can. We would hold the wire handle and twist it back and forth until Mama would open the can and scrape down the sides. This made it freeze quicker. Meanwhile, Papa had gone to Hickory, MS in the wagon and bought a whole 24-bottle case of RC Cola, peach and grape Ne-Hi drinks, and a big hunk of bologna and cheese. Man, we had a ball under the four oak trees in the yard. Three of them are still there. Lightning struck one the day your grandfather died. Last, but not least, Papa had marked the first watermelon that came on the vine, so he would know which one was ripe for the fourth of July. That is the day the first watermelon was pulled and put in a tub of cold water so it would be cool when we cut it. Those were the best days- "I do not want to go back too, far, just remember."

Dr. Gill Davis Newton Eye Clinic

Joe Alexander, Owner
Alexander's Hardware

William Alexander, Owner
Alexander's Hardware

Lana Buckley

Taylor Corley (and his girlfriend)

Verlanda

To Davey my son:

This being my last book, there are so many things I want you to know. I am so proud to be your mother. You are the light of my life. The Lord saw fit to take Melvin & Arthur (the sons I miss so much) away from us. I can not tell you the whole story because it is so unusual. I hope that is the right word to use. So I will put it another way. God gave me another son. A man that had already been taught to love God by loving people. I knew his mother & father had prayed that he would have a good life when He saw fit to take them to a better place. God gave this loving man to me. I am so proud to be called Mama Earline by him. When you are in other countries working, he makes sure I am o.k. I want you to call him when you need a brother. You can depend on him. I know, because he promised me he would be there for you. His name is Glenn Parker. You will find a cake I made up and named The Glenn Parker Cake in this book. His band plays at the Beau Rivage in Biloxi, MS.

Davey, let me tell you where you came from because I can not tell you where you are going. You must set your own goals in life.

Mattie Edison

This is your grandmother on my father's side. My love for cooking came from Mattie Edison. I remember she stopped people who passed by her house and said, "Stop and eat. I just cooked some peas and bread and made a cake." Davey, she would take one egg and make a cake that would melt in your mouth. She cooked cakes for everybody, white and black, for $1.50. Davey, she made it up by hand. There was no electricity. She made icing by beating it with a fork. It was always perfect. Her meringue stood high.

Now, today, 76 years later, I need at least 8 eggs and an electric mixer. I get $30.00 dollars for my cake and still fail sometime. Your great grandmother lived on what is now Highway 15; only a dirt road then. She lived on the Rozey Farm. The Rozey Descendants are still living there on Highway 15 just before you get to the Southern Pine Light Company. She lived on the right side of Highway 15 going north which is now pastured land.

Now for your great grandparents on my mother's side. My grandmother said she was an only child. She never knew her father. She remembered when she was about 6 years old, standing on a block along with her mother, being sold to a man named Sutton. She grew up as Betty Sutton. She never went to school, but she was smart, wise, and intelligent.

Betty Levy, 1856 - 1952

Filmore Johnson, 1854 - 1945

Davey, she made all her clothes by hand. I wish everyone could have seen the short stitches she made when she was sewing. She made most of her clothes out of fertilizer sacks and flour sacks. She made her underclothes with the flour sacks because the material was soft. The fertilizer sack had a number or writing on them. I remember one sack number very well: 6.8.8. She would wash it with soap she made up herself. I know some of the things she used to make the soap: the ashes from the fire place, if we had burned oak wood that day. She would save some in a bucket until she was ready to make her soap. She never used pine wood ashes only oak! We never knew why. She also used Red Devil Lye. Red Devil Lye is stronger than anything I can tell you about (maybe acid) just to give you an idea. She called it Lye Soap. She would boil those sacks in an iron pot until they were white as snow. Sometimes, it took 2 or 3 boilings to get them like she wanted them (white). She made her skirts, blouses, panties and slips. She called them petticoats.

Davey, she wore her apron to church starched and ironed. She made her starch out of flour and water. She always made two pockets on her apron. All her grandchildren tried to sit next to her in Sunday School because we knew she had some homemade tea cakes in her apron pocket. If we were good we'd eat tea cakes when church was out. Davey, she died at age 104 years old. I was fourteen years old when she died.

Now, your grandfather was Philmore Johnson, my mother's father. Back then, he was what you would call today, a pimp. I hate to tell the world, but you must know the truth. He was mean as Hitler. He died at age 96 when I was about 12 years old. I knew him and his two brothers. Davey, he told us that he and his two brothers were sold into slavery to different families. He knew his mother and father. He knew all three brothers and lived around Hickory, Mississippi when they got old because they kept up with one another. My grandfather and his brothers all could read. My grandfather was a Johnson. Your cousin, Robert Johnson, the richest black man in the world, is his grandson. He now owns the NBA Bobcats basketball team. His brothers were raised as Petrey and one Uncle Preston. I remember all three.

I could tell you more. This is enough to let you know you must stand tall. Don't attempt to make yourself ask God to make you what you ought to be. You should live by His rules and not man's. Love people. Treat people like you want to be treated, you don't have anything in your background to be ashamed of, unless it's your mother who picked cotton until cotton left this county (smile). Let these words live through your daughter, Loran, my grandsons, Christopher and Melvin (Poochie) Shipp, and last but not least, my God-given son, Glenn Parker. And don't forget Kenneth (Fire Truck) Jones, my steak cooker and friend. I love you, Fire Truck.

Earline Edison Broomfield

13

Some Things I Know
Not Revealed by Man

1.   *God is Real.*
2.   *To know for yourself what God wants, you must
     humble yourself. You must ask God, Jesus, the
     Holy Spirit, whatever you want to call Him, to
     open spiritual ears so you can hear. Read God's
     word, then listen. God is a revealing God. He talks
     through nature and other people. I can not tell you
     how many ways He talks, son. Do try Him around
     midnight on your knees, some people say in your
     closet. I want you to understand, so I say, shut
     the world out. Tell Him what you want, if you need
     it, God will give it. There is so much I want to tell
     you, it is impossible, so you must seek Him for
     yourself.*

3.   *God sees about His children on time, because He
     is a timely God. He may not come when you want
     Him, but He is always on time.*

   *Davey, this book is dedicated to you, but I do hope some-
one else will get something from this writing. Jesus saved me in
1977. I thought I knew so much about the Lord. I attended the
McKinnely Seminary for years, taught by some great ministers.
Man, you have never been taught until you are taught by God,
our Lord and Savior Jesus Christ Himself. I learned more in May,
June and July 1999, than I did the 67 years I'd lived. Davey, God
is real. He was real all through a heart attack, son. I give up, I
can not write all I know. Seek Him for yourself.*

                                        Love,
                                        Mom

DAVEY AND GLENN
When you get my age, look for this...

Old folks are worth a fortune with *silver* in their hair, *gold* in their teeth, *stones* in their kidneys, *lead* in their feet and *gas* in their stomach.

I have become a little older since I saw you last. Today is December 4, 2008. Your mother is 79 years young and holding. A few things have changed in my life. Frankly I have become a frivolous old gal. I am seeing five gentlemen every day!

As soon as I wake up, **Will Power** helps me get out of bed. Then I go to see **John**. Then **Charlie Horse** comes along, and when he is here he takes up a lot of my time and attention. When he leaves, **Arthur Ritis** shows up and stays the rest of the day. He doesn't like to stay in one place long. He takes me from joint to joint. After a busy day, I'm really tired and glad to go to bed with **Ben Gay**. What a life.

P.S. The preacher came to call the other day. He said at my age, I should be thinking about the hereafter. I told him, "Oh, I do all the time. No matter where I am - in the parlor, upstairs, in the kitchen or down in the basement." I ask myself, "Now what am I here after?"

(copied)

I LOVE YOU!

Mother And Son

Remember This...
A Recipe On Life

1. An investment in knowledge, always pay the best interest.

2. The way to get started is to quit talking and begin doing.

3. For success, attitude is equally as important as ability.

4. A cloudy day is no match for a sunny disposition.

5. Success is a ladder you cannot climb with your hands in your pockets.

6. Anything unattempted remains impossible.

7. Being willing makes you able.

8. To get what you want, stop doing what is not working.

9. A champion is a dreamer that refused to give up.

10. Excellence is doing ordinary things extraordinarily well.

11. The best way to predict the future is to invent it.

12. Last but not least - Tough times never last, but tough people do. (copied)

What is it?

It is greater than God;
More evil than Satan;
If you eat it, you will die;
The rich don't need it;
The poor got all they need.

Answer: Nothing

Given to me by Jimmy Pender, Campers on Mission

**Davey, you asked me to write some more history
in my final pages. So, here it is.
To my sons Davey Doby and Glenn Parker, my grandsons
Christopher McDonald and Melvin (Poochie) Shipp:**

Mr. Rudolph Ellis

Today is August 24, 2008. This is my final book. I want you four to know I love you so much. You have given me so many happy years. I thank you. Davey, I never told you about the poor house. When I mention the poor house, my customer's say they thought I was talking about their house. I am giving you a little history of where you came from. There was an old man who lived in the community named Henry Bennet. His granddaughter and I were good friends. They lived next door. Now I told you my grandfather was mean as Hitler, but my grandfather was a saint compared to Uncle Henry. He was not my uncle, but we had to call him that because he was so old. I hate to say this, but you talk about ugly! All of us kids was scared to death of him! One day Uncle Henry disappeared. Mama told us he was in the poor house. We did not know where the poor house was. I did not care so long as he was gone. Now the reason I wanted him gone was when mama and papa bought a 10 lb. sack of flour, the merchants would give them a pretty plate or bowl. We kids would claim the pretty ones. My plate was so pretty with pretty red flowers. One day when I came home from school, Uncle Henry was eating out of my pretty plate. (Davey you know where I grew up because you bought the home place we owned. We had a 2 class room school at the church.) I think I cried all night because Uncle Henry ate out of my plate. Mama told me she washed it good and she promised to whip me if I did not shut up. And when she told you, you was going to get a whipping she meant it. But papa came to my rescue. He told me I did not have to eat out of that plate again and I never did.

Davey, I never found out where the poor house was. We thought it was in Jackson, MS, seventy miles away. My white son, Rusty McMillian did some research and guess what? It was in Decatur, MS about ten miles away. I don't ever remember going to Decatur. It was too far away. I did not know anything about Decatur, MS. I really found out about Decatur when I went to high school in Newton, MS. Then I learned it is the town they called the county seat. All state and local business was taken care of in Decatur. This is where the big jail house was. Davey, when I was young, I only know of one man that went to jail and he was out when I heard about it. It was a disgrace to go to jail. Now in your time it seems that you are not popular unless you go to jail. There are thousands in jail today.

Now, back to the poor house - The Poor House was a place provided by the state. They had one house for black and one for white. They say it was terrible and if the health department was like they are today, they would have burned it to the ground.

Davey, I did not know I was poor. Your grandpa and grandma never told us we were poor. If we was poor, everyone in Hickory, MS was poor because everyone had the same thing - two mules, a wagon, two cows, maybe ten hens, and one rooster. Mama cooked all the roosters while they were fryers, I mean about 6 to 8 weeks old. When we sat down by the fireplace at night to study our lesson, our little bellys were full of peas and bread and buttermilk. We did not get much whole milk, which you call milk. I do not remember if you ever tasted buttermilk. When my brothers milked the cows, mama would strain the milk through a white flour sack (which she kept to strain the milk and nothing else). You did not use or touch her milk straining rag. Davey, she kept it white as snow. She placed the milk in a container which was called a churn. You don't see me, but now I am in tears.

Sunday night, November 10, 2008, it came to my mind that I am talking to a man who graduated from Hickory High School, East Central Junior College, and Alcorn State University, Lieutenant Colonel of the United States Army, going all over the world teaching environmental health and safety, OSHA, D.O.T., E.P.A., and only God knows what else. Growing up- as my grandma would say- you are poor as a snake, but I am so proud of you because I know you milked cows at Alcorn State University to help me get you through. But when you walked up to get your diploma and the man said, Davey Charles Doby (Magna Cum-Loudy). I don't know what he meant, but I was still proud. (smile) I said all this to let you know I still know more than you. I lived history.

Now, back to the churn. The milk stayed in the churn overnight, so it would sour. Then we would churn the milk until the butter came to the top of the milk. Remove the butter. Now you got buttermilk. So, we had buttermilk and bread anytime you wanted it.

So, Davey, if we went to our cousin's house to play we had the same thing. If my brothers went to a white neighbor's house to work, they had the same thing. Your grandfather never sent me and your aunt Maudie out to work because we had 6 brothers to go. He kept us at home to do the work like pick cotton, and chop the cotton to remove the grass. Davey, we had to keep all the grass cut out of the yard. I mean clean and then sweep the yard with what we called a brush broom. There is a special tree that grows that we used. It still grows all around us. When you come home ask me and all I'll have to do is look out the window to show it to you. Now that is not all it was used for. When mama took one limb away from the broom, brother you got your (B) tore up and the police did not come! You never did that same thing again!

Davey, my job at home was - listen to this - keep all the grass cut out of the yard, sweep it up in a pile, burn it or throw it away in the woods. Now today, in your time, we plant the grass in the yard, and if there is a bare spot, we set grass out. We get mad if someone walks on it. We fertilize it to make sure it is pretty and green and grows. Then we cut it to keep it pretty.

Here is another dumb thing - I know my older readers will get a laugh out of this because they know what I am talking about. My father would plant the corn seed about 12 inches apart. He dropped the seed by hand. Sometimes he would drop more than one seed in case one did not come up. Or sometimes there was a mistake and some fell too close to one another. Now when the corn came up, we had to take a hoe and walk every row to remove the one little corn plant that was too close. Young people, ask your grandparents what I am talking about. Now today Davey, they sow the seeds. My day, one seed every 12 inches. Your day, at least 10 seeds every 12 inches, and this makes so much more corn. Look how far we have come. I shall take you farther.

Frankie J. Johnson

Mama and I stayed in the field working until about 10 a.m.. My sister Maudie was staying in Newton with my Uncle Percy, your grandfather's brother. She had finished the 8th grade so she had to go away to high school in Newton, MS. Mama and I would cook dinner, we called it 12 o'clock daytime dinner. You call it lunch. We cooked enough for supper, which you call dinner. What will they call it when they open up Davey's Country Cooking Cookbook one hundred years from now? They placed one of my cookbooks in a capsule and buried it in the Montrose community in Louin, MS to be opened one

19

My father, Edd Edison

hundred years from 2001. Maybe they will call it EAT. The kind of food I cook today no doubt will be gone forever.

Davey, we had to go to Newton, MS to live with someone else. Every Sunday, rain or shine, sleet or snow, papa would hitch up the wagon and take us about 10 miles to school to board with another family all the week. And we would be packing food to take with us like flour, corn meal (which we had taken to the griss mill from corn we had raised ourselves), a little bag of sugar, a box of sweet potatoes, (which we had grown,) and our own home made molasses - all we wanted. We always had plenty of that because we had plenty of sugar cane. We had enough to last all week most times. We three got 25¢ each. I mean one quarter, and had a dime left to catch the train back to Hickory on Friday. Sometimes papa would meet us in Hickory, but sometimes we had to walk the 6 miles home. We were the country kids because maybe at that time there were two or three hundred people who lived in the town of Hickory. Big deal. I told you what people call poor. I want you to always remember that money does not make you rich. Let me tell you what will make you rich.

Number one, know Jesus. Don't think you know Him. Know that you know Him. Know that you know God the Father, Son and Holy Spirit. You got peace of mind when you: go to bed at night not afraid, have a portion of health and strength as grandmother used to say, when you got food to eat, family and friends that love you, and are able to tell your neighbors you love them. These are just a few things that tell you are rich, because money can not buy any of these things. So my son, richness is not money. I know I am rich now and have very little money. But there is no one in this world more happy than your mother. Know my secret. Know Jesus.

Now sometimes I wonder how papa sent three of us ten miles away to go to high school. To give you an idea, remember the "Little House On The Prairie Show"? We went to a school like that one. One teacher taught everyone in the same room, one grade after the other. If it was not your class, you sat still or went out to play and I mean quietly. I would like to see someone try that today. (smile)

My parents never told us we were poor. I still live in a house. I still eat peas and bread. I did move up from Kool aid to iced tea. (Big deal!) As grandma used to say, I still have a portion of health and strength. Boy am I rich!

I know how to survive when things get tough. Davey, I know you saw a black man become the President of this great country in which you lived in 46 years. I know it took me 79 years to see it happen.

20

TO DAVEY DOBY AND
GLENN PARKER

Today, January 13, 2009 is my final message to you in this book. (I love you!) I want you to know the most admired business people who were always taking interest in my work and I believe tried to help by being kind and doing just small things to help. No. 1 Mrs. Carolyn Buckley, Jasper Co. News; Mike Butler, Newton Piggly Wiggly and Sid Williams, Williams Brothers Grocery in Philadelphia, MS. I want to thank them and want them to know I appreciate them so much, Davey.

Glenn Parker

If God had blessed me with a daughter, I would have wanted her to be just like Shirley Parker. When I got Glenn Parker as a son, I got my daughter through his wife.

Davey, I have always wanted a bible school to teach people about Jesus Christ - He is the President of the whole world. I want my readers to think about this... sometimes we go to church and Satan is never mentioned. Satan is the one that messed up the world. He starts in the home. As a baby, if he is not taught at home, he will go out in the world and then, boy oh boy!

When I was a young girl, I remember reading a book called "Dealing With the Devil". I have asked people about the book, but they have never heard of it. It starts off with two ministers who took a trip by car to a convention in another state. When they arrived at the convention, the man who was with him messed up everything. Nothing was right. When he realized he had brought Satan to the convention, he was inspired to write the book "Dealing With the Devil". Today, I am asking all mothers and fathers when you teach your children about Jesus, tell them about Satan too. He is the DECEIVER.

A few months ago, my brother Rev. Oliver Edison, walked into the kitchen at Davey's Restaurant. We were getting behind with our lunch because the oven kept going out. The ladies had given up on lighting it. He asked what was wrong. We told him the oven would not stay lit. The pilot kept going out. He stood still and these are the words he said. "Satan, you get the hell out of this kitchen! We don't have time to fool with you today!" We lit the oven and it did not go out again. So today when we have a problem, we say, "Satan, not today." We must learn how to identify Satan and stop him now. He cannot stand the name of Jesus Christ. But he never stops trying. He never gives up.

My favorite young people - I admire them so much because of the way they act. Chris Sims, Miles Henry, Brittney Lindsey, Madeline Logan, Landry McMullan and last but not least, Joshua White. My final message to you and to all my customers all over the world...

I LOVE YOU AND MAY GOD BLESS AND KEEP YOU!

Love,
Earline Edison Broomfield

Mr. & Mrs. Brodie & Lori Myrick and Family

Davey, I know I have been trying to name the last cake I put together for over a year. November 4, 2008, at ten minutes past 10 p.m., I got the name for my last cake when the man on TV said Barack Obama will be the next President of the U.S.A. I will be sending him a book when it comes out - the United States best.

THE OBAMA CAKE

1 box Duncan Hines Devil's Food Cake Mix
1 box Duncan Hines White Classic Cake Mix
2 cans coconut pecan icing
1 cup vegetable oil
8 eggs
1 cup milk
1 cup evaporated milk

Mix cake mixes together. Add eggs, oil and milk.
Mix with electric mixer until smooth and
creamy. Fold coconut pecan icing into cake
batter. Beat and mix well with spoon.
Pour into two large round cake pans or two 9 x 13
cake pans. Cook at 350⁰ or until cake springs
back when touched by hand in center

ICING:
1 can Duncan Hines Milk Chocolate
1-1/2 cans Duncan Hines Classic White

Mix icings together to get the perfect color. Stack first layer of cake and ice, then sprinkle with chopped pecans. Stack second layer on top of first layer and ice entire cake. Place pecan halves around bottom edge of cake. Sprinkle top and sides with chopped pecans. Good and pretty!

As I close, Davey Doby and Glenn Parker, remember today you can be whatever you want to be. If you don't believe me, ask Joe the plumber or Barack Obama!

I love you!
Mama Earline

Strange Old Lady Takes Over My Life

A very weird thing happened. A strange old lady has moved into my house. I have no idea who she is, where she came from, or how she got in. I certainly did not invite her here. All I know is that one day, she wasn't there, and the next day, she was. She is a clever old lady, and manages to keep out of sight for the most part, but whenever I pass a mirror, I catch a glimpse of her and whenever I look in the mirror to check my appearance, there she is, hogging the whole thing, completely obliterating my gorgeous face and body. If she insists on hanging around, the least she could do is offer to pay part of the rent, but no. Every once in a while, I find a dollar bill stuck in a coat pocket, or some loose change under a sofa cushion, but it is not nearly enough. I don't want to jump to conclusions, but I think she is stealing money from me. I go to the ATM and withdraw $100, and a few days later, it's all gone. You'd think she would spend some of that money to buy wrinkle cream. Lord knows she needs it. And money isn't the only thing I think she is stealing. Food seems to disappear at an alarming rate - especially the good stuff like ice cream, cookies and candy. I can't seem to keep that stuff in the house anymore. For an old lady, she is quite childish. She likes to play nasty games, like going into my closets when I'm not home and altering my clothes so they don't fit. And she messes with my files and papers so I can't find anything. She has found other imaginative ways to annoy me. She gets into my mail, newspapers and magazines before I do, and blurs the print so I can't read it. She has taken the fun out of shopping for clothes. When I try something on, she stands in front of the dressing room mirror and monopolizes it. She looks totally ridiculous in some of those outfits, plus, she keep's me from seeing how great they look on me. Just when I thought she couldn't get any meaner, she proved me wrong. She came along when I went to get my picture taken for my driver's license, and just as the camera shutter clicked, she jumped in front of me! No one is going to believe that the picture of that old lady is me.

Author Unknown

"I Hope This Little Cookbook Will Bring Smiles and Joy to Our Customers Long After I Am Gone"

Keith Sims and grand daughter Lexi

Especially to our regular customers: the Peco Boys, Kíp, Todd, Russ, Mike and Scott (Red). Last, but not least: Big Phil Scott and my friend Keith Sims, who's happy with fresh cabbage, a chicken breast or stuffed bell peppers, along with his son Chris, daughter Leah and his mother, Mrs. Sims.

Jack Upton

We shall never forget Jack Upton and Terry Lee Simmons, my favorite punching bags. BAD, BAD, BAD. Jolene Page, restaurant pest, along with Katie Watkins Jones, often accompanied by Judge Jessie Bender. Also Wesley Hendry and son Milus.

We shall never forget Jerry and Margie Halerison, who drove 90 miles round-trip to eat at Davey's Restaurant and visit with me and my customers. Jerry and Margie are part owners of Lady Forest Chicken Plant and Farm.

We call my friend Mr. Barney Jones, "man not choosy, just feed me."

Julia and Wison Welborn

My favorite customers, Mr. and Mrs. Welburn, from Sharon, MS missed very few Sunday dinners. I called him "the peasheller man" because he invented his own pea sheller and sold them throughout the south, along with his wife Julia, that old woman who I love dearly.

Ralph Cahill

John Sims, my no. 1 pest and beat 3 supervisor in Jasper County, ate here also. No. 2 pest is Willie B. Barlow, who ate when he wanted to and paid for his food when he had to, which was not often.

Thad Moncrief, which I call Jack my handy man as long as there was no work in the job! He would run errands all day, but not work.

25

His excuse, "my breath is short" (emphysema). My little friend Mr. Wesley was a good friend of my brother Ardell. Every visit, his grandson Darrell accompanied Mr. Wesley. I almost forgot Shea (Alcorn Student), her mother Mrs. Chester Gavin and the Smiley brothers G.W., H.B. and Leroy.

The Buckley Children

Can't forget my special friend, Mr. John Calvin Simmons, who's food was put in his truck by one of the workers or me, for at least seven years. His son Brent Simmons and his wife ate their wedding supper at Davey's Restaurant, as well as Mr. and Mrs. Harry Smith of Montrose, MS.

Davey, I can not name all of my many customers. People from all walks of life eat at Davey's. These are just a few more of the people I served almost everyday. I know I will miss someone, but I love you too. Men from the Newton County Bank No. 1, Mr. Bill Freeman, Doug Whittle Jr., Mr. Mason, along with the man who loved breakfast, Rusty McMillian and daughter Landry.

The famous blues singer **Percy Sledge** loves my candied yams and fried fish. His most popular song is "When a Man Loves a Woman."

On September 26, 2000, I had a special guest for lunch, Mr. Taylor, weatherman from Hattiesburg, MS, along with four friends from WDAM TV. He talked with me, the workers and several customers.

Others who came pretty regular were lawyers Bill May, Robert Logan and Newton Mayor. Can not forget M.L. Moffett from Ellisville, MS, Mr. Ham Batty and wife, also Willie Mae Jordan and her husband. Congressman Chip Pickering also enjoyed a good meal at Davey's.

John Soley & Friends

26

CHIP PICKERING
THIRD DISTRICT
MISSISSIPPI

September 26, 2000

Mrs. Earline Broomfield
5628 Highway 15
Louin, Mississippi 39338

Dear Earline,

I can not thank you enough for the enjoyable lunch I received at Davey's Half Way Home Café . All of your staff were delightful. but your service was exceptional! I can not remember a time when I have had such marvelous fried pork chops and sweet potatoes! Maybe on my next trip there, I can try your one of your specialities, the bar-b-que ribs or the catfish. My time with all of you was definitely a treat.

Again, my thanks to you. Your hospitality and generosity were greatly appreciated. If you are ever near Washington D.C., please let me know. With warm regards and best wishes, I am

Sincerely yours,

Chip Pickering

Best Wishes -
Thank for your
great cooking & hospitality

Dr. Paul A. Little of Brandon, MS was a frequent customer, as well as Highway Commissioner, Wayne Brown of Lucedale, MS and Dr. Samuel H. McLaurin, dentist in Bay Springs, MS.

Silena Williams and Rose Keller, my two best friends were always there for me. Mrs. Lee Hollinsworth of Lake, MS was a good friend also. Mr. and Mrs. Jack Crosby, Mr. Edd Nelson, Jack's brother-in-law, had to take care of our little monkey for years. Davey, you will never figure this one out. This is a joke between Jack, Edd and me. I worked with these two for 25 years and every day was an adventure along with "Price Brooks."

On February 4, 2001, the TV Star of "Mississippi Outdoors, " Melvin Tingle, ate at Davey's Restaurant.

Davey, 90% of the good meat served at Davey's Restaurant was purchased from this group at Gavin Piggly Wiggly, Newton, MS.

"A special edition from my hospital stay on July 31, 2009"

To my son Davey, and my adopted son, Glenn Parker with a special kind of love, to grandsons Christopher McDonald Shipp, and Melvin (Poochie) Shipp III: I promised you I would not write another book, but I feel like God is not finished with me yet and I am so thankful. I know my job is to cook and tell the story about my contact with Jesus Christ. As I lie in my hospital bed, many thoughts went through my mind: One, my special friends and customers: Dr. Shelby Thames, and his sons Dr. Scott Thames and Dr. Clay Thames. Today we made a special pie called "Dr. Dr. Dr. Thames Coconut Pie" from Earline Broomfield's Recipe:

1 cup of sugar, ½ cup of all-purpose flour. Mix well. Add 2 cups of milk, one half stick of margarine, 3 egg yolks (save white for topping), 1 teaspoon vanilla and 1 ½ cups of coconut. Mix well. Pour into deep-dish pie crust, which has been browned in oven. Beat egg whites until stiff. Add ¼ cup of sugar. Pour over filling. Sprinkle with coconut. Brown in oven. Ready to serve.

Dr. Shelby Thames, Dr. Clay Thames, Dr. Scott Thames

Dr. Clay is my favorite. Dr. Scott is jealous of his younger brother. I got you Dr. Scott. Ha Ha.

Let us go back when I was about six years old. My father was always fixing crosscut saws. He always sharpened saws for customers. One day I bent over and cut my knee. It bled for a long time. He finally poured kerosene over my knee to stop the bleeding because it was a favorite medicine of my time. It was always good and it still is. Davey, I must start telling things about our life when we grew up. I grew up with 6 brothers and 1 sister. We never had to plow a mule, but my brothers did. We had boys to plow the horses and milk the cows when we were kids. The main job for us was to watch honeybees come over the house and through the yard. We had to make noise too. Mama and Papa always kept old plows, old buckets, and pans to beat on. The queen bee could not hear or communicate with the other bees. No one knew what the queen bee would do. We would keep up so much noise the bees could not hear, so they had to come to a big, big ball of bees, all stuck together in one pile because they had to light on a limb or a small tree or the ground when the bees had to stop. My father would build what you call beehives. He would build a box about 3 feet tall and about 1½ feet wide. He would place this box over the bees and tap on top of the box until all bees went up into the box. Then he would cut a small hole in the side of the box so the honey bees could come in and out to begin collecting pollen to make honey. We never saw the queen bee but Papa said she was always there because there was always one queen in every beehive. When a new set of bees come to hatch and come out, a new queen was hatched out. She would always be the first one to hatch. Sometimes there would be 10 or 12 new queen bees. My father said time they were born, the new queen would kill all the other queens before their eyes came open because they could only have one queen bee in the hive. They would live close to our farmland smelling the flowers and collecting pollen to make honey. In the fall of the year, my father would rob the bees and take honey away from the beehives into the house, cut the honeycomb into small pieces, place it in a sack and let honey drip through a pretty white sack until it had all dripped out. He would place the honey in jars or jugs; therefore, we could skip eating molasses and eat hot biscuits with honey for a while and chew the honeycomb like gum. Davey, it was a good time to make up so much noise to stop the bees. One day my brother Johnny saw the whole swarm of bees go into a pattern. He stopped because they had nowhere to land. He was running so fast, that he ran into a small pine tree. The bees were trying to stop on his head, he barely escaped. They stopped on a tree. My father came up and built a beehive and took them home. I always wondered how many bees would be in one hive with all her followers, must be thousands and thousands at one time.

Now Davey, it is about time we grow up, but I always remember some things new, so let me tell you about a little doctoring my mother and father did. For the last few years, I have been showing all my friends a plant. It was a grass plant. It saved so many people from getting sick. One was called fever grass. It had green leaves like grass. The roots looked like yellow gold. Every spring of the year, mama would wash the roots and boil it to get every youngin' in the house 1/2 cup of tea. The more sugar she put in it, the bitter it got, but you only needed it one time because everything left went out our stomachs. Then there was a mullet tea. You see it sometimes along side of the highway. Mama or grandma would boil the mullet making tea. Sometimes she would boil green pine straw to make a tea to drink for a bad cold. We were never sick. Sometimes they had to get the doctor because someone had pneumonia. The doctor always rode in a buggy. He got paid with a little money, and would also get eggs or a hen or rooster or some fresh kill hog meat, maybe a ham. Alright, now lets talk about the real herbs. When we were kids, my grandma took us down in the pasture where we had a spring with running water. Let us call it a springhead. It was always wet in the pasture. She set out some plants along where the water was always damp. She called this plant a calamus root. It has grown on our land I know over 79 years. We hardly ever get calamus root now. We just let it grow. I know my brother Clifton, 84 years old now, set out some plants in Pennsylvania to watch them grow. When he moved back to the old home place, he started pulling it (the root) up again so he could set out some more plants. In a year's time, you have a little patch of the roots running two or three inches apart. Now you can pull up the root out of the ground, wash it

Diamond Keyes

30

clean, scrape off all the roots that look like mini roots along the main root and cut them off. If the root gets dry, it gets hard like a stick. Now if you eat certain foods like spicy foods, and have heart burn, upset stomach, gas, or if young women are pregnant and sick on the stomach like morning sickness, it is gone the minute you put it in your mouth and swallow the juice and keep the root in your mouth. You are well within minutes. One day one of my workers came in and told me she was sick. Her name is Precilla, we call her Skitter. She wanted to go home. I told her to put a piece of calamus root in her mouth. She did so. She forgot she was supposed to be sick. She went back to work. This was about 7 years ago. The cook always keeps her calamus root for other people. Now one day a young woman came in with her husband and two small children. She came into the restaurant but she was too sick to eat. She had morning sickness. She spoke to me and said, "Ms. Earline, I am so sick. I cannot eat." I asked her if I could give her something to take to make her feel better. She told me, "Ms. Earline, I would trust you with anything." I gave her a small piece of calamus root, told her to hold it in her mouth, to swallow the juice, not the root. The minute it touched her stomach, she looked at me and said, "I'm not sick anymore." She could not believe it. She came back one week later talking about calamus root. Now I give so many people calamus root to hold in their mouth. The only place I know, where the plant is located is my family's land six miles south of Hickory, Mississippi in the Good Hope community. My grandma's name was Betty Sutton Johnson. She died at the age of 104 years old and also used the plant.

Davey, I must leave you a small note on one young man that worked here in the restaurant. His name is Ronald Hardy, we call him New Yorker. He moved back to Montrose, Mississippi from New York City. He told me how his mother ate dirt. There is a certain type of dirt here in Mississippi so many women eat. You can find it in places like the bank side of many dirt roads in Mississippi. His mother loved to eat dirt. When you dig the dirt from the bank sides, it looks like clay. There would be no grit mixed in with the clay. My friend New Yorker wanted people to know his mother ate dirt. The dirt had a distinct smell, which women love to taste and eat. It is something you get from nature because you knew nothing in the store to satisfy you or your taste buds.

Ronald Hardy (New Yorker)

Now let's go back to Possum, Squirrel and Rabbit hunting. So many times we did not have pork or beef meat to eat. But most times we did have some type of wild game meat to eat. Papa and my brothers would go out at night in the woods and catch possums. Sometimes we had a lantern, sometimes we had a lighter knot, which was a fat piece of wood you could start a fire with within minutes with a match. They would hold it up high in trees and look for a possum. They also had a carbide light on their cap which you could see up in the top of trees. They would let the dogs out at night, find the possum, climb the tree, knock him out, put him in a sack, and head for home. The first thing we would do is put him over a fire and burn all the hair off him and scrape him like a hog. Remove all hair, wash him very clean. Remove his insides and throw it away. Wash the possum clean. Leave him in salt and water inside a bowl overnight to remove some of the wild taste away. Then we placed him in a pot full of water with salt and pepper, boiled him until tender. Remove him from the pot, place in a baking pan. Save some juice left from boiling the possum. Turn the possum skin up. Place strips of bacon over possum, bake until brown, boil sweet potatoes in water until half done. Place the sweet potatoes around possum and finish baking. (He is opossum, but we call him possum). So many times we fried the opossum. You may bake coons the same way, but you must clean him different. He must be skinned to remove all hair. About six months ago in 2009, a man called Walt Grayson wrote about my coon cooking and banana pudding in the Mississippi newspapers and TV.

Many people have my first cookbook. I have received many letters about cooking coons from my recipe in the first cookbook. My brother and I was talking the other day about fishing in our small branch that runs through our pasture. We fish with a string because we did not have a fish line. We never had a fish hook. If we had an extra fish hook, mama always used it, but we always used a straight pin. Take a straight pin, bend it back halfway. Take a string; tie it around the small head of the pin. Take a small nail to use as lead. Rake crawfish from the branches and small puddles of water. Catch crawfish as bait to fish with. Use only the crawfish tail. Fish all day with a straight pin. Now it is time to cook fish and make fish gravy. Here is the recipe:

Clean the fish. We call them red bellies and perch, small catfish. In my day we used lard made from hog meat. Use just enough lard to fry fish in a skillet. When the fish is done, remove fish. Add corn meal to the skillet. Stir until thick and crumbly. Add salt and a little black pepper and cook until brown like corn meal. Fish and fish gravy is ready to eat on corn bread or biscuit. We never had much white bread. The fish and gravy was so good and our little bellies was full with buttermilk. Today, 80 years ago, we could not afford many fish hooks. Maybe five hooks for a nickel. Today I know everyone, even I, think we were stupid. But God fed us and kept us safe. Now it is time for tears. My God still lives and helped Dr. David Sullivan forever checking on your mother's heart and blood condition.

Davey, there are things that you must always remember. There were people that brought me through life, good and bad. It was Jesus' love that brought me to the world. My mother and father taught me so many important things about life. So many good people gave me a helping hand. There were many outstanding people in the community that had a positive impact on my life, such as Professor N. H. Pilate, the principal of my high school in Newton, Mississippi, a man named Troy Brand, Newton McCormick of Hailey's Hardware in Newton, Mississippi. I can remember Dr. Horace May, my mama's first eyeglass doctor. His son, my friend

Lawyer Bill May would always have his Big Thanksgiving dinner from Davey's Restaurant. We would always fix the meal and deliver it to his residence. Lawyer May must have sweet potato casserole. My Lawyer, Robert Logan, the first lawyer

Bill May

I ever talked to about law business, would always eat at the Restaurant. He is still a tightwad. Never forget Lawyer Marvin Oats always gave me free advice, and my first eye doctor was Dr. Gil Davis. Two men looked out for me always: Rusty McMillan and Charles Holder. Today, December 22, 2009, my good friend William "Bill" Freeman had lunch with me. I have known him all his life and he

Robert Logan

has touched my life so many times and ways. He has done so much to help me support my three sons. He was a banker. Now he is a Major General in the Mississippi National Guard. He is truly a good friend. I will never forget these great men in my life.

The two greatest men in my life are Davey Doby (son) and Glenn Parker (adopted son). Davey, I want you and Glenn Parker to print this book like it should be printed. I must not forget my two little angel friends always sitting waiting for me and ready to help out when I need them, always ready to do a job for me, my two best little friends Madeline Logan and Landry McMillan along with their mothers. To close my book, some of the greatest men that walked through Mississippi: Sid Williams, Co-Owner William Brothers General Merchandise, Rusty McMillan, Robert Logan, Bill May, Charles Holder, Mike McNeil, G. W. Smiley, Richard

Mike McNeil, Charles Holder (Hol-Mac) & Rusty McMillan

Headrick, O. J. Edison, Bill Freeman, Cliff Edison, Ronnie and Zack Buckley of Buckley Newspapers & family, Michael Buckley, Rev. Cleveland Hayes, Senator Haskins Montgomery, Keith Sims, Wesley Hendry, Mike Butler, and Glenn Johnson, my mama's favorite nephew because he was always ready to take care of my mother "Aunt Nootsie". Representative

Landry McMillan & Madeline Logan

Johnny Stringer, Lee Upton, Craig Bird, Pat Kirby (Dragline), Doug Whittle, Mike Gieger, Lonnie Thigpen, Lonnie Phillips,

Major General Bill Freeman, Adjutant General Mississippi National Guard

Representative Johnny Stringer

G.W. Smiley

Mr. Wesley Hendry & Grandchildren

Tommy Williams, the Blakeney boys (Keith, Kendrick, and Kevin), Harvey Curry, Carter Sims, Joseph Sims, Morgan Sims, Shelton Culpepper, Jay Baucum, the Holder boys (Chuck, Jamie, Jeffrey, and Rory Dale), David Glaser, Lawyer Ricky Ruffin, Gray Swoope, Mark Ishee and son. I must not forget Dr. Mark Norton. Whenever I

Charles Holder

meet him, I see Dr. Jesus along with Dr. Luke. So many times I addressed Dr. Mark Norton as Dr. Luke. Now there's time for more tears. Last but not least, Ms. Carolyn Buckley, Rose Keller, and Shirley Parker, my best stand-by's in the world, along with my friend and a great singer Frankie Bennett, along with a piece of chocolate pie. Cheryl Bostic from Hutto, Texas is a special friend.

Davey, I have been ill about 5 weeks so I started writing again because God is not finished with me yet. So many people are asking me to and I do not know where to start. I made a big move a few days ago. I moved into an apartment building with all senior citizens, old folks like me. Everyone I've met is so friendly. We are not senior citizens. We are just old folks. I write in this book when I think of things. It was about two weeks ago, I met a man at the restaurant called a councilman from the Indian reservation. I met his wife and son. His son was such a friendly young man who just became a doctor. He was so interested in the old folks things his mother and I was talking about in our conversation. His mother asked me did I know or remember how to clean and cook hog brains. Many younger folks have never heard of this; so here is this recipe for you (smile) because it has been 60 years since I cooked them but I never forgot how. Once my father killed a hog, he removed the brain with one handful all together and put them in a bowl, poured lukewarm water over

Harvey Curry, Newton, MS Chief Of Police

Kinley Hoover

them, and pulled a thin membrane off the brain, placed them in a skillet, and cooked slowly with a little shortening, stirring until they begin to foam like soap. Cook and stir until they look well-done. Add

Carter Sims

Sid Williams

raw eggs into the brains and cook them. They look like scrambled eggs with salt and pepper. When ready to eat, you have enough scrambled eggs and hog brains for at least 8-10 people. Serve with

Shelton Culpepper

hot biscuits and syrup. They tasted very good back then when we were kids. You can still find them canned in a grocery store in Mississippi.

Davey, I remember when your Uncle Ardell went into the army in World War II in 1941. My brother Chester and Clifton went to the war a few months later. Three brothers were gone at once. My mama stayed up day and night, and always cried. My brothers sent

Rick and Frankie Bennett

the family allotment government checks from their salary. Therefore, when we went to school, the special thing my father did with the money was have my brother Oliver James Edison and my teeth fixed. Man, we even had gold in our mouths,

which lasted for years. I remember Mama's favorite prayer, I must stop now and shed some tears. Mama's words was always, "God bring my boys home, and I will trust you the rest of my life." She took these words home with her, trusting God the rest of her life. I lost two brothers years later, but my brother Clifton is 84, in good health and still plants all my vegetables at Davey's Restaurant. My brother O. J. and I are still here but my older brother Cliff always keeps a blue cup in his hand every day, but I do not know what's in that cup (smile). Davey, one day you ask your uncle what's in that cup?

David Glaser

All my brothers went to war, but your uncle O. J. was also in the Korean War. Now when President Kennedy was killed in '63 I believe, I was picking cotton in the field. A few months later, I was the eighth black woman hired in the Newton Company

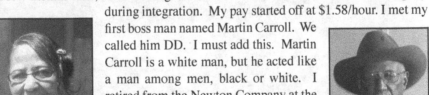

Rose Keller

during integration. My pay started off at $1.58/hour. I met my first boss man named Martin Carroll. We called him DD. I must add this. Martin Carroll is a white man, but he acted like a man among men, black or white. I retired from the Newton Company at the age of 62. Davey, a few months later, I opened a small restaurant in Newton, MS. I was open for 4 years in a store behind the chief of police named Chief

Oliver James Edison

Mowdy. Seven months later I reopened and moved to Jasper County. I stayed in Davey's restaurant for 18 years. You will not believe this, I never had a problem in Davey's restaurant. I never had to call a

Policeman or Highway Patrolmen. They always came to the restaurant only to eat. Now, only time for more tears.

Davey, six months ago, in 2009, I did have a problem. A woman, a little tipsy and two of her friends, came to the restaurant for Friday steak night. They tried to cause trouble in the restaurant. They were saying everything on menu was too high. Two of my customers and good friends, named Lance Garvin and Billy Grayson chased them out of the restaurant. I also remember, I got two speeding tickets in my life. One, when I was running late at the Newton Company. Years later, in Jasper County, from one highway patrolman named Ralph Smith who ate at my restaurant. Ralph is now retired from the Highway Patrol. I got by without paying the ticket. Ralph had to pay me for the cookbook and I was so glad his picture was in the 4th edition. I made him pay me back. He is holding a pie in his hand.

Davey, I must go back some years later to my first restaurant in Newton, MS. Mr. Bill Freeman, vice-president of Newton County Bank, Rusty McMillan (my white youngin'), Lawyer Bill May, and Lawyer Robert Logan (Tightwad—always asked for a hotdog), but I only cooked pork chops, chicken, bread, cakes, and pies.

Let's talk about a little witchcraft. Something happened in the sky, which we never did like. I remember it so very well, I remember this happening about 3 times in my 80 years on this earth. I watched what we called witchcraft. About a year ago, my friend and I, Rose Keller, were coming out of Meridian Mississippi. A dark cloud came up. We stopped because we were afraid of the bad weather. We cannot say who we saw because my friend never saw this as I watched the cloud. It split wide open. One part went one way. The other part went another. The rain stopped while we watched. About 12 years ago, Rose Keller, who is not as old as me came into Davey's Restaurant. My grandson Chris was there also. We sat there and watched a terrible dark cloud come up in Montrose, MS. A woman took a hatchet, walked outside, and struck the hatchet down in the ground. The dark cloud split open. One side went one way. The other side went another. When this happened, I fired the woman and did not let her come back in the restaurant. I saw this 3 times in my life. It happened when I was a child. Our next door neighbor was passing by our house one day. A dark cloud came up. She picked up the axe, cut down in a stick of wood, and she kept walking. The cloud split open. The rain was gone, and it is the truth. This is too deep for me. I cannot explain what happened because I don't know what happened, but it is the truth. Two people witnessed this incident at the restaurant. This was Rose Keller, and my grandson Chris McDonald. I never want to see this witchcraft again. (smile) Davey, I finally met a woman of 84 years old named Sarah Temple and she told me she saw her father split clouds so many times. I still say, you stay away. (smile)

Davey, I never saw you smoke a cigarette, I have never seen you take a drink of whiskey, or say a bad word in my house. You have been a good man, the kind I love to talk about. Well, if you have ever been to jail, I did not know anything about it. I know you have done something, but I never saw it. Thank you Davey.

Love, Mother.

I must say a few words to Mike Strebeck and his son, a young doctor, who took time to see about me when I got sick in the restaurant. Thank you. Dr. Strebeck, I have a lot of respect for your future. Your daddy loves my fried apple pie. If I ever needed anything from the store, I got it on credit. (Smile)

Davey, my boyfriend came a few weeks ago. He stopped and left me a ring and a note. He met me at the restaurant, a man that did a lot of wildlife hunting. Every year, he was the first man to kill a turkey, clean it, and bring it to the restaurant for all the customers. His name was Dickey Dickson. We could not cook wildlife at the restaurant unless it was inspected by USDA. We cooked the wild turkey outside the restaurant. He came by and bought me an engagement ring because it was my birthday. He is my white boyfriend. He and his wife come to see me and have lunch with me. His wife is a lovely lady.

As I close, I know a deerhunter and his sons, named Patterson. He hunted at least

15 years around here and ate his lunch with me. He had a son about 8 years old and everyday he wanted cheese toast. Sometimes, I would give him a funny look, but he still said I want cheese toast. So now I always call him Cheese Toast. But now he eats like his father and brothers. I have a lot of respect for you, Mr. Patterson and your sons.

Davey, my son, you can go back down through history and see how God has blessed this family down through generation after generation. Although my grandmother, Betty Sutton Johnson was sold into slavery when she was 6, she lived a full life and died at the age of 104.

Davey Doby and Glenn Parker, I love you.

Davey, I know you took care of me. The secret is after I met Glenn Parker, I never bought any more clothes. He and his wife bought me everything. Yes, God has been good to me!

Mama Earline

Dickie & Donna Dixon

Mike Strebeck, Owner Western Auto, Newton, MS

TO SERVE 100 PEOPLE

Coffee . . . . .3 lbs.
Cream . . . . .1 qt.
Milk . . . . .6 gals.
Fruit Juice . . . . .4- no. 4 cans / 26 lbs.
Soup . . . . .6 gals.
Meat Loaf . . . . .24 lbs.
Beef . . . . .40 lbs.
Hamburger . . . . .36 lbs.
Wieners . . . . .25 lbs.
Ham . . . . .40 lbs.
Roast . . . . .40 lbs.
Chicken Pie . . . . .40 lbs.
Potatoes . . . . .35 lbs.
Vegetables . . . . .4- no. 10 cans / 26 lbs.
Baked Beans . . . . .5 gals.
Cabbage (slaw) . . . . .20 lbs.
Fruit Cocktail . . . . .2-1/2 gals.
Rolls 200
Bread . . . . .10 loaves
Butter . . . . .3 lbs.
Potato Salad . . . . .12 qts.
Vegetable Salad . . . . .25 qts.
Fruit Salad . . . . .12 qts.
Salad Dressing . . . . .3 qts.
Pies 18
Cakes 8
Ice Cream . . . . .4 gals.
Loaf Sugar . . . . .3 lbs.
Whipping Cream .4 qts.

To Serve 50 People, divide by 2
To Serve 25 People, divide by 4

NOW THE RECIPES FOR THE BEST TASTIN' FOOD IN THE SOUTH

SALADS

SOUTH EASTERN FUNDRAISING

Ralph Cahill & Ms. Earline Broomfield

Davey's Best Cooking in the South

ANNA CLAIRE DAVIS
PASTA SALAD

Pasta
4 cucumbers
1 12 oz. pkg. cooked ham
1 12 oz. pkg. cooked turkey
2 small cans sliced black olives
2 cups grape tomatoes, cut in halves

Cook your desired pasta until well done. Drain. Cut ham and turkey in cubes. Peel cucumbers and cut lengthwise in four pieces. Cut out seeds and discard. Cut cucumbers in small pieces. Mix all together and pour 16 oz. bottle italian dressing over pasta mixture. Place in refrigerator until ready to serve.

CORN SALAD

2 Cans shoe peg whole kernel corn
2 medium tomatoes, chopped
1 medium onion, chopped or diced small
Salt and pepper to taste
1/2 cup mayonnaise

Mix all ingredients together and serve.

CABBAGE SLAW

1 small cabbage head
2 whole carrots
½ cup sugar
½ cup mayonnaise
4 tsp vinegar

Grate cabbage and carrots together. Add sugar, mayonnaise, vinegar and mix well. Place in refrigerator until chilled.

TUNA SALAD

3 cans tuna, drained (prefer tuna packed in spring water)
6 boiled eggs, diced
4 T. hotdog relish
1 small apple diced
1 stalk celery chopped fine
¼ cup mayonnaise
½ cup chopped onion (optional)

Mix together all ingredients. Keep in refrigerator covered. Serve on crackers. Makes great sandwiches on toast with lettuce and tomatoes.

EARLINE'S POTATO SALAD

10 lb. bag white potatoes or any Irish potato
1 1/2 small jars hotdog relish
1 cup mayonnaise (or enough to hold together)
½ cup sugar
½ tsp. salt
½ tsp. black pepper
1 tsp. garlic salt
12 boiled eggs

Peel and cut potatoes in medium cubes. Boil in salt and water until tender but firm. Strain in colander. Pour cooked potatoes in mixing bowl. Chop or slice boiled eggs over potatoes. Add hotdog relish, mayonnaise, sugar, pepper and garlic salt. Stir all together. More or less sugar may be used. It's good hot or cold.

YOUR OWN GARDEN SALAD

1 medium lettuce head, separated and washed
   under cold running water (set aside to drain)
2 medium to large tomatoes
6 round red radishes
2 cucumbers, peeled and sliced

Chop or tear lettuce in medium size pieces in large bowl. Add all other vegetables and toss together. May be served with boiled eggs and tender green onions. Use your favorite salad dressing.

CABBAGE SALAD

1 small cabbage grated
1 small carrot grated
2 small boxes raisins
1 apple chopped
1 cup chopped pecans
¼ cup vinegar
½ cup sugar
1 cup mayonnaise

Mix well and keep covered in refrigerator until ready to serve.

3 Sisters - Lynda Ford - Tillman, Earnestine Ford & Dorothy Chapman

MY MAMA'S CHRISTMAS AMBROSIA

10 apples
10 seedless oranges / remove seeds, if any
2 whole fresh coconuts
1can fruit cocktail
1 can peaches
1 cup sugar

Peel apples and remove core. Peel oranges. Open coconut and peel off outer dark skin. Open fruit cocktail and peaches. For best results grind all together in old fashion meat grinder. Food chopper may be used. Add sugar and stir. Keep in refrigerator until ready to serve. Serve over pound cake. Good about 2 days.

EARLINE'S CABBAGE SLAW

2 medium size cabbages
2 carrots
½ cup sugar
½ cup mayonnaise
4 T. vinegar

Grate first three ingredients. Add sugar, mayonnaise, vinegar. Mix well. Keep in refrigerator until ready to serve.

BREADS

To Davey, My Son

When my life on earth is finished
Miss me, but let me go.
When I come to the end of the road
And the sun has set for me,
I want no rites in a gloom filled room.
Why feel sad for a soul set free?
Miss me a little, but not too long
And not with your head bowed low.
Remember the love we once shared?
Miss me, but let me go.
This is a journey we all must take
We all must go alone.
It is all a part of the Master's Plan,
One more step toward home.
When you are lonely and sick at heart,
Go to the friends we know
And bury your sorrows in good deeds,
Miss me, but let me go
Because no mother has had a better son
than you have been to me.

(copied)

I Love You,
Mama

CORNMEAL PANCAKES

1 cup cornmeal
¾ cup boiling water
¼ cup flour
½ tsp. salt
2 eggs, beaten
½ cup milk
2 tsp. baking powder
3 T. melted shortening

Pour the boiling water over the cornmeal and let stand 5 minutes. Add the flour and salt and mix until free from lumps. Combine the eggs, milk and beat into the cornmeal mixture. Add the baking powder and shortening, beat well. Drop by tablespoonfuls onto a hot griddle or frying pan with oil. When the pancakes brown on one side flip over and brown on the other side. Serve with jelly or syrup.

CREAM OF WHEAT CORN BREAD

2 cups Cream of Wheat
½ cup self rising flour
1 tsp. baking powder
2 eggs
¼ cup milk
¼ cup vegetable oil

Mix all ingredients together. Pour in greased baking pan. Bake at 350 degrees until golden brown, about 30 minutes. (My mama says this delicious bread is good for people suffering from ulcers. It is good for the whole family.)

Never burn the bridge you cross; you might have to cross back over the same side you came from

EARLINES NIGHT TIME PANCAKES

2 cups flour
2 tsp. baking powder
¼ tsp. salt
1 T. sugar
1 egg
1 ²/₃ cups milk
2 T. melted shortening

Sift the dry ingredients together. Beat the egg lightly and add the milk. Pour onto the flour mixture. Mix and beat well. Add the shortening. Heat griddle or skillet and lightly oil with vegetable oil. Cook the pancakes, turning the pancakes when they are full of bubbles and brown on bottom. Turn and brown on the other side. Serve with syrup, honey or jelly.

ANNIE LOIS' MAYONNAISE BISCUITS

3 ½ cups self rising flour
1 ½ to 2 T. mayonnaise
Enough milk to make the dough

Mix well. Put dough on a cookie sheet and cut out. Place on greased pan and bake in 400 degree oven until golden brown. When brown, spread butter on top of biscuit and serve.

Chastity Windham & Elmyra Payton

HUSH PUPPIES

2 ½ cups corn meal
1 tsp. salt
2 tsp. onion flakes or ½ cup finely chopped onion
¾ tsp. soda
1 ½ cups buttermilk
butter or oleo

In a medium bowl combine corn meal, salt, onion flakes or chopped onion, soda. Add milk and mix well. Heat fat or oil (1 inch) to 375 degrees. Drop batter by spoonful into hot fat. Fry until brown, about 2 minutes. Serve hot with butter or seafood.
NOTE: Oleo is the same thing as margarine.

CORNBREAD FRITTERS

1 cup self rising corn meal
¼ cup of milk
¼ cup self rising flour
1 egg
1 T. melted shortening

Mix all ingredients together. Drop by tablespoonful into a hot frying pan slightly greased. When the fritters are brown on one side, turn over and brown the other side. Serve hot.

Doug Hill & Jimmy D. Reynolds, Narcotics Agents

BANANA NUT BREAD

2 cups sugar
4 eggs
2 cups shortening
1 cup chopped pecans
2 ½ cups flour
6 over ripe bananas
3 tsp. soda
dash of salt

Kenny Jones, Steak Cook

Combine all ingredients. Bake at 350 degrees to 375 degrees for 1 hour. Seems better if frozen awhile.

Maudie Massey

LAST MINUTE ROLLS

1 ¼ cup scalded milk
2 ½ T. sugar
1 ½ tsp. salt
¼ cup soft shortening
1 pkg. Yeast or cakes
¼ cup warm water
3 ¼ cup sifted flour

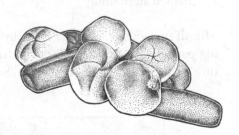

About 1 1/2 hours before dinner, pour scalded milk in large bowl, stir sugar, salt, and shortening. Cool until luke warm. In small bowl, sprinkle or crumble yeast into warm water. Stir until dissolved. Stir into luke warm milk mixture. Add flour; stir until well blended, about 1 minute. Cover with towel and let rise until doubled. Knead dough. Fill greased muffin pan cups or pinch off and put in pan. Bake at 400 degrees for about 25 minutes. Makes 1 dozen.

Sharron Williams

HOMEMADE BISCUITS

4 cups flour
4 tsp. baking powder
½ tsp. salt
½ tsp. sugar
4 T. shortening
¾ cup milk

Sift the dry ingredients together. Work in the shortening with the back and edge of a spoon (I use a spatula). When flaky add the milk. Turn on to a slightly floured board. Pat or roll into ½ inch thickness. Cut biscuits with a biscuit cutter or a glass dipped in flour. Place on a slightly oiled pan. Bake at 450 degrees, about 12 minutes.

DIFFERENT CORNBREAD

2 cups chopped onion
¼ cup oleo
1 8 oz. sour cream
1 cup cheddar cheese
1 ¼ cup self rising corn meal
1 T. sugar
2 eggs, beaten
18 ¼ oz. cream corn
¼ cup milk
¼ cup vegetable oil

My best friend, Randy Corley

Saute onion in oleo until tender. Let cool. Stir in sour cream and ½ cup cheese. Set aside. Stir together remaining ingredients and pour into lightly greased 9 inch pan. Spread sour cream mixture over top and sprinkle on remaining cheese. Bake in 375 degree oven until done.

QUICK DONUTS

1 can biscuits
½ cup, sugar
½ tsp. cinnamon
Deep fat fryer

Cut hole in biscuits with bottle top or pointed knife. Drop biscuits and biscuits holes in deep fryer. Cook until golden brown. In brown paper bag add sugar and cinnamon. Shake bag to mix well. Add hot donuts to bag and shake to coat donuts and holes with sugar and cinnamon. This may be done in your regular skillet with enough vegetable oil to cover donuts.

BAKING POWDER BISCUITS

4 cups self rising flour
1 tsp. baking powder
½ tsp. sugar
¼ cup, shortening
1 ½ cups milk

Sift the dry ingredients together. Work in the shortening with the back and edge of a spoon. When flaky add the milk and mix well. Turn dough on to a floured board. Pat or roll to one half in thickness. Cut with a biscuit cutter or glass. Place in baking pan. Bake at 400 degrees for 12 to 15 minutes or until golden brown.

Highway Patrol man, Tracy Boyd, wife Denise & Mrs. Earline

CRACKLIN' BREAD

2 cups self rising corn meal
1 cup self rising flour
1 T sugar
2 eggs
1 ½ cups milk
2 ½ cups cracklings
1 heaping T. mayonnaise

Sonny Jones

Soak cracklings in hot water for about 10 minutes. Mix all other ingredients as if making regular corn bread. Add crackling. Bake in a 400 degree oven about 30 minutes or until done.

CORN BREAD

Same as crackling bread. Leave off crackling and add ¼ cup, vegetable oil.

HOME MADE BAKING POWDER BISCUITS

3 cups flour
3 tsp. baking powder
½ tsp. salt
½ tsp. sugar
3 T. shortening
¾ cup milk

Sift the dry ingredients together and work in the shortening with a spoon or finger tips. When flaky add the milk. Turn onto a floured board and pat or roll to ½ inch thickness. Cut with a biscuit cutter or glass dipped in flour. Place in baking pan. Cook at 450 degrees for 15 minutes.

Don't count your chickens before the eggs hatch

UNBELIEVABLE FRIED GRITS

Use leftover grits, about 2 cups. Add 1 egg, salt and pepper to taste. Add enough flour to thicken, to resemble uncooked cornbread. Heat enough butter in skillet to fry like pancakes. Drop grits in skillet and brown on both sides. Serve with bacon and eggs.

COOKED GRITS

To serve good grits, cook in enough water so you will not have to add water when grits begin to cook. Add butter and salt when grits begin to boil. Cook grits 15 to 20 minutes. The longer they cook the better they taste.

JALAPENO CORNBREAD EARLINE STYLE

3 cups self rising corn meal

1 cup self rising flour

½ cup mayonnaise

2 cups whole kernel corn

1 T. sugar

1 cup grated cheese

1 cup jalapeno peppers cut or sliced

½ cup vegetable oil

3 eggs

1 cup milk

Mix all together, cook in muffin pan at 350 degrees until golden brown.

EARLINE'S BISCUITS

3 cups self-rising flour
1 tsp. sugar
¼ cup shortening
1 cup milk

In large bowl, mix flour, shortening and sugar together using finger tips or spoon until looks like corn meal. Add milk stir until all come together. Pour on floured cutting board. Mix in flour to form a dough ball, roll out half and place in oven. Bake at 350 degrees until golden brown. Brush biscuits with butter while hot.

MR. BIG JOHN FLAP JACKS

1 ¼ cup self rising flour
2 T. sugar
2 eggs
2 T. vegetable oil

Mix all together beating well with large spoon. Cook in skillet or grill slightly greased at medium temperature. Brown one side turn over brown other side. 1 large spoon full will make 1 flap jack.

Bruce Riley & Jimmy Grayson

EARLINE'S FLAPJACKS

2 cups all purpose flour
1 cup milk
1 T. sugar
2 T. vegetable oil
½ tsp. baking powder
2 eggs

Mix all ingredients together. Drop batter by spoonful on lightly greased griddle or iron skillet. Turn when bubbles appear. Cook other side until golden brown.

FRENCH TOAST

2 eggs
1 cup milk
2 tsp. sugar
1 pinch salt (⅛ tsp.)
¼ tsp. baking powder
10 slices stale bread (optional)

Mix first 5 ingredients together. Dip the bread slices in this custard mixture and drain. Brown on a hot griddle or iron skillet that has been oiled well. Serve hot.

OLD FASHION CORNBREAD

3 cups self rising corn meal
1 cup self rising flour
1 T. sugar
3 eggs + 1 cup milk (or more if necessary)
¼ cup cooking oil

Mix all ingredients together with enough milk to make batter look like cake dough. Cook in greased skillet or pan at 425 degrees or until brown.

ORANGE BISCUITS

1 large can biscuits
1 stick margarine or butter
1/2 cup orange juice
1 cup sugar

Mix 1 stick of margarine or butter melted, 1/2 cup orange juice, and 1 cup of sugar. Place biscuits in juice. Bake as directed.

Glenn Parker Band

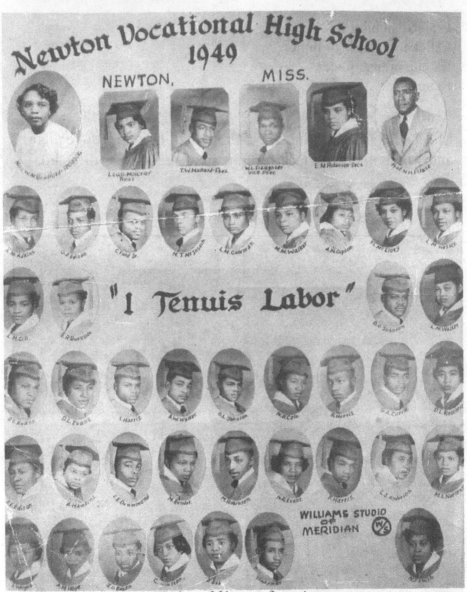

Newton Vocational High School
1949

NEWTON, MISS.

"1 Tenuis Labor"

WILLIAMS STUDIO of MERIDIAN

Ms. Earline; fifth row, first picture

VEGETABLES
SIDE DISHES

CHILDREN!!!

TIRED OF BEING HARASSED BY YOUR STUPID PARENTS?

ACT NOW

MOVE OUT, GET A JOB
PAY YOUR OWN BILLS...
WHILE YOU STILL KNOW
EVERYTHING.

(copied)

FANCY GREEN BEANS

2 pkgs. frozen French-style green beans
1 can water chestnuts, thinly sliced
2 T butter
1 can cream of chicken soup
1 pkg. frozen French-fried onion rings
Parmesan cheese

Cook beans until tender. Mix soup, chestnuts and butter with the cooked beans and put in a casserole dish. Place the onion rings on top with the parmesan cheese sprinkled over all. Bake at 300 for 30-40 minutes.

Gladis Pace

SQUASH CASSEROLE

1 quart squash, cooked and drained
1 stick margarine
1 cup cracker crumbs
1 can cream of mushroom soup
1 cup grated cheese
1 small onion, chopped
Salt and pepper to taste

Layer half of the squash in casserole dish, then half onion, half cracker crumbs and half soup. Continue to layer these ingredients until all are used. Top with margarine and then cheese. Cook in 400 degree oven for about 30 minutes.

Gladis Pace

FRESH STRING BEANS

Remove both tips from beans. Break in desired lengths or about 2 ½ inches long. Prepare Dutch oven or heavy pot with pieces of ham. Wash beans in cold water and place beans in pot. Add butter or margarine, salt and pepper. Stir regularly over low heat. Beans will make own juice. Cook until tender.

POTATO CASSEROLE

8 medium potatoes
2 cans cream of chicken soup
1 large onion grated
½ lb. sharp grated cheese

Cut potatoes in chunks and par boil. Drain potatoes, add soup, onion and cheese. Season with salt and red pepper. Put in casserole dish and dot with butter and more grated cheese. Bake at 350 degrees for 45 minutes. Freezes well. Makes 8 servings.

Gladis Pace

PEPPER HASH

1 dozen red pepper
½ cup brown sugar
15 medium onions (red skin)
3 T. salt
4 T. vinegar
Black pepper to taste

Grind onions and peppers, cover with hot water and let stand over night. Add brown sugar, salt and pepper. Cover with vinegar and heat thoroughly. Do not boil. Store in sterile jars for future use. A tasty relish for all meats and fowls.

Mary Ruth Farmer

BAKED BEANS

1 gal. canned baked beans
¼ cup brown sugar
½ tsp. black pepper
1 cup catsup
1 lb. ground beef

Cook ground beef in skillet. Stir until crumbly. Drain off excess grease. Add all ingredients together. Bake in 350 degree oven until hot and bubbly. Serves 20.

GREEN BEAN CASSEROLE

3 cans whole green beans
1 small carton sour cream
1 can cream of mushroom soup
½ stick margarine
24 salty crackers
1 lb. package Velveeta cheese
Garlic salt

Drain beans. Spread over bottom of oblong baking dish. Sprinkle with garlic salt. Mix sour cream and soup. Spread over beans. Cut cheese into thin strips. Put layers on top of mixture. Crush crackers and mix with margarine. Spread over cheese. Bake in 300 degree oven for 30-45 minutes until thoroughly heated.

Gladis Pace

SPICY VEGETABLE CHILI

1 can tomato soup
1 can creamy onion soup
2 soup cans water
1 - 16 oz. can chick peas (garbanzo beans)
1 - 16 oz. can black beans, rinsed and drained
2 medium zucchini coarsely chopped (2 cups)
2 medium carrots coarsely chopped (2 cups)
1/2 tsp. dried thyme leaves, crushed
1 T. chili powder
1/8 tsp. pepper

In 4-quart sauce pan combine soup and water. Stir in chick peas, black beans, zucchini, carrots, chili powder, thyme, pepper. Heat to boiling. Reduce to medium heat. Cook 40 minutes. Stir occasionally.

Mary Ruth Farmer

SQUASH CASSEROLE #2

2 cups cooked squash
¾ stick butter
1 tsp. salt
1 cup grated cheese
2 cups mashed cracker crumbs
1 cup cooked onions
2 eggs
½ tsp. pepper
1 cup evaporated milk

Chad Parker, MS Highway Patrol Man

Cook squash and onion together. Mix with other ingredients. Place in casserole dish and cook at 375 degrees about 40 minutes.

Gladis Pace

EASY BROCCOLI BAKE

1 can cream of broccoli soup
¼ cup milk
1 tsp. soy sauce
1 (2.8 oz.) can French fried onions
1 bunch fresh broccoli, cut up or 1 20 oz. package frozen broccoli,
   cooked and drained
Dash of salt

In 1 ½ quart shallow casserole, combine soup, milk, soy sauce and pepper. Stir in broccoli and ½ can of onions. Bake at 350 for 24 minutes or until hot. Stir. Top with remaining onions. Bake 5 minutes.

Gladis Pace

FRIED GREEN TOMATOES, SQUASH OR CUCUMBERS

Wash and slice vegetables about 1/4 inch thick. Pour 1 cup milk and 1 egg over vegetables. Coat well. Remove vegetables. Roll in 1 part corn meal and 1 part self-rising flour. Season with salt and pepper. Deep fry or brown both sides in skillet.

Earline Broomfield

FRIED WHITE POTATOES

Wash and slice potatoes about ¼ inch thick. Pour 1 cup milk and 1 egg over vegetable. Coat well. Remove potatoes. Roll in self-rising flour. Season with salt and pepper. Deep fry or brown both sides in skillet.

SPICY POTATOES

½ pt. carton sour cream
8 oz. cream cheese
½ tsp. garlic powder
2 T. chives
½ tsp. salt
Butter, black pepper to taste
Paprika, sprinkle on top

Cook and mash potatotes, add soft cream cheese, sour cream and other ingredients. Put in casserole dish and sprinkle paprika on top. Bake at 350 degrees for 35-40 minutes or until hot and bubbly.

Gladis Pace

CHILDREN ONE DISH MEAL IN 15 MINUTES

2 cans pork & beans
½ lb. ground beef
1 tsp. sugar
¼ cup catsup
Dash salt and black pepper

In skillet brown ground beef stirring until crumbly. Drain off fat from ground beef. In same skillet, add pork and beans, sugar.

HOLIDAY YAM BAKE

1 40 oz. can yams
18 ½ oz. can crushed pineapple and/or raisins
2 T light brown sugar
2 T. butter or margarine melted
3 T chopped pecans
¾ cup miniature marshmallows
Pam cooking spray

Drain yams, mash well. Drain pineapples, reserve juice. Add juice to yams. Add sugar and butter and beat well. Stir in pineapple and pecans. Coat inside of 1 ½ quart casserole with Pam. Spoon in mixture. Bake for 20 minutes at 350 degrees. Sprinkle with marshmallows. Bake for 10 minutes longer. Serves 8.

Clementine Bruce

MACARONI AND CHEESE

3 lbs. macaroni
1 lb. cheese
1 quart sweet milk
6 eggs
½ tsp. black pepper
1 tsp. salt

Add macaroni to boiling water. Cook until done but not mushy. Pour macaroni in colander and rinse with running hot water. Pour macaroni into baking dish and place sliced cheese on top of macaroni. Mix next four ingredients. Pour over macaroni and cheese. Bake in oven until milk and cheese mixture congeals. Serve hot.

Tracy Giles, Ann Frazier, Joe Tally,
& State Rep Haskins Montgomery

FRESH TOMATO GRAVY

4 ripe tomatoes
3 T. all purpose flour
1 tsp. sugar
4 T. meat drippings
Salt and pepper

In sauce pan slice tomatoes and cook in 2 cups of water until tender. Set aside. Using an iron skillet, add meat drippings and heat until hot. Add flour, salt and pepper, stirring until it makes a smooth brown paste. Slowly add tomatoes and sugar. Let boil until it looks like gravy. Serve over hot biscuits or rice. You can make this gravy by using canned tomatoes or tomato paste.

STUFFED BELL PEPPERS

5 lbs. ground beef
4 cups cooked rice
4 eggs
½ cup milk
1 tsp. garlic salt
¼ tsp. meat tenderizer
1 tsp. black pepper

Mix all ingredients. Cut 10 bell peppers length-wise. Remove pulp and seeds. Rinse. Stuff peppers and place in large pan. Bake in 350 degree oven until meat is done. Drain off excess grease. Heat 3 large cans mushroom spaghetti sauce, 1 cup water, ¼ cup sugar. Pour over pepper. Simmer 15 minutes. Serve hot.

Bobby Butler

FRESH FRIED OKRA

Remove stem from okra. Wash and let drain. Cut okra in about 1/2 inch pieces. Mix corn meal and 1 part plain flour, just enough to coat the amount of okra you are frying. Add salt and pepper to taste. Heat about 1/2 cup oil or shortening in skillet or frying pan. Cook over medium heat until okra browns. Turn over with spatula. Brown other side or until okra is tender. Remove from pan and serve. For Davey's Restaurant touch, cut a few fresh hot peppers in okra before frying.

BLACKEYED PEAS

2 lbs. blackeyed peas
¼ cup ham pieces
1 tsp. salt
2 tsp. sugar
1 small onion chopped (optional)
1 stick oleo
2 qts. cold water

Wash dry peas in cold water. Put peas in favorite cooking pot. Add all ingredients at once. Cook about 1 hour or until peas are tender.

CANDIED YAMS

10 medium or 8 lbs. peeled sweet potatoes, cut in 2-inch round
   slices or length-wise. Set aside.
4 cups water
4 cups sugar
½ lb. margarine or butter
1 tsp. nutmeg

Boil first 5 ingredients until they look like syrup. Add sweet potatoes. Cook until tender.

74

BABY LIMA BEANS OR BUTTERBEANS
FRESH OR FROZEN

3 lbs. beans
1 tsp. salt
1 tsp. sugar
1 stick oleo
¼ lb. sliced ham

Richard Beasley, Warlery, Ohio

Place beans in boiler. Add enough water to cover beans, about 1 inch of water over beans. Add next 4 ingredients. Boil until beans are tender.

BIG BATCH FRESH CREAMED CORN

18 ears cut-off corn
¼ lb. butter or margarine
½ tsp. salt
½ tsp. black pepper
2 T. sugar
½ cup all purpose flour
2 cups water

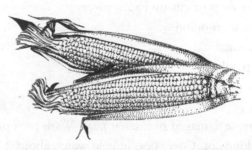

With a sharp knife, cut corn about half way off the grain, cutting from one end of the cob to the other end. Then scrape the cob. This is where you get the creamed corn from. In a large heavy pot or stainless steel pan, add next 6 ingredients. Mix well. Cook in oven until corn is creamy and bubbly, about 1 hour.

FRIED SWEET POTATOES

Peel and wash sweet potatoes. Slice in about ¼ inch slices. Fry in butter over medium heat. Brown on both sides. Cook until tender. Drain off excess fat. Sprinkle with a little sugar and ¼ cup water. Steam until sugar melts.

CANNED STRING BEANS

1 gal. cut green beans. Do not drain. Add small pieces of ham slices.
1 ½ T. sugar
½ tsp. salt
2 cups water
½ tsp. black pepper
1 stick oleo

Mix all ingredients together. Cook over medium heat about 30 minutes.

DRY BLACKEYED PEAS

3 lbs. blackeyed peas
Ham slices or cut-up bacon pieces
1 medium onion
1 T. sugar
1 tsp. salt
¼ lb. margarine

Remove damaged or broken peas. Wash peas in cold water. Place in desired cooking pot. Cover peas in cold water, about 2 ½ quarts. Add all ingredients. Cook until peas are soft to touch about 30 minutes.

FRIED ONION RINGS

2 ½ cups flour
2 eggs
1 cup milk
½ cup water
vegetable oil or fat

Peel and slice onion. Chill in refrigerator (optional). Mix flour, eggs, milk and water. Dip onion rings in batter and fry in deep fat until brown. This batter is good for fried shrimp and oysters.

FRIED SQUASH~ GREEN TOMATOES, EGGPLANTS, CUCUMBERS

Wash and cut into rounds, abut 1/4 inch thick. Mix 1 egg and 1 cup milk together. Place whatever you have to fry in milk and egg wash. Mix 1 cup corn meal, 1 cup self-rising flour together. Place whatever you are frying in corn meal and flour mixture, coating well. Drop in deep hot oil, one at a time. Cook until brown.

SWEET POTATO PONE

Grate about 6 medium to large sweet potatoes

Add:
1 ½ cups sugar
½ cup molasses
1 cup milk
1 tsp. nutmeg
½ tsp. salt
3 eggs

Mix all ingredients together. Pour into greased baking pan. Bake until potatoes will not shake, about 30 minutes at 325 degrees.

COUNTRY FRIES

In iron skillet, heat vegetable oil about ¼ inch in diameter. Peel potatoes. Cut into large pieces and sprinkle well with salt and pepper. Cover skillet and cook potatoes on medium heat until brown on one side. Flip over and brown other side. Keep turning potatoes until all potatoes are tender. For extra goodness, cook with coarsely chopped onions.

SWEET POTATO CASSEROLE

4 cups mashed sweet potatoes
1 ½ cups sugar
1 stick oleo
1 cup milk
1 tsp. vanilla flavor
1 tsp. nutmeg
¼ cup raisins (optional)
3 eggs

Delores (Edison) Graham/Kennedy
and son, Crandal Kentae Graham

Mix all ingredients with electric mixer. Pour into casserole dish. Bake until done in 350 degree oven.

Topping: Cover casserole with marshmallows. Put back into oven about 5 minutes or until marshmallows brown.

FRESH CUT COLLARD GREENS

Pick, cut and clean collards. Wash in cold water until trash and grit are gone. Place into stainless steel pot. Put just enough water to keep from sticking in winter. Add several pieces of ham, ham hocks, bacon grease or lard. Collards cooked in summertime require more water and more cooking time. Add salt and fresh jalapeno peppers. Stir regularly. Cook until greens are tender. All greens are best cooked in heavy bottom pots or stainless steel. Not just any pot will cook good greens.

Turnips may be cooked the same way. Just add more water. Turnips must boil longer than collards. Leave off hot peppers.

For cabbage, use oleo instead of bacon grease or lard. Leave off hot peppers. Cabbage may be cooked with ham hock juice. Boil ham hocks until done and add juice to cabbage. Add same ingredients as turnips.

BIG BATCH FRESH STEWED SQUASH

10 lbs. squash
2 sticks oleo
4 large onions sliced
1 teaspoon salt
½ tsp. black pepper or to taste
½ cup water

Wash and cut squash into ½ inch rounds. In heavy pot or iron skillet add squash and oleo, salt, pepper and water. Cover with lid. Cook squash until it makes its own juice. Uncover and add sliced onion. Cook until squash begins to brown slightly.

LAZY MAN'S CORN ON THE COB

Place unshucked corn in the microwave. Cook for 5 minutes. Remove shucks. Add salt and butter. Very good and juicy.

UNCOOKED MIXED PICKLES

Fresh cucumbers, fresh bell peppers and young, tender fresh okra. Quarter cucumbers. Cut bell peppers in ½ inch strips. Leave okra whole. Place in clean, grease-free bowl. Add ½ cup salt, cover completely. Let stand over night. This will make its own water. Wash away all salt. Mix 60% vinegar and 40% water. Pour over pickles. This will stay in refrigerator. Crisp for months.

Lexi Sims

LAWYER BILL MAY
SWEET POTATO CASSEROLE

5 medium sweet potatoes
3 cups sugar
2 sticks of butter or margarine
6 eggs
½ tsp. nutmeg
1 tsp. vanilla flavor
¼ cup chopped pecan (optional)
½ cup evaporated milk
1 bag marshmallows

Cook sweet potatoes in skin until soft. Cool with cool water. Peel potatoes and set aside. While still warm, add butter or margarine. Beat with electric mixer until smooth (no lumps). Add eggs, nutmeg, vanilla flavor, and milk. Mix well. Sprinkle baking dish with chopped pecans if desired. Pour sweet potato mixture over pecans. Bake at 300 degrees until firm. Place marshmallows on top of casserole. Brown and serve.

OLD FASHION TOMATO GRAVY

4 T. meat drippings
3 T. flour, all-purpose
Salt and Pepper
1 teaspoon sugar
1 can whole tomatoes (mashed)

Using a cast iron skillet, have the drippings hot. Add flour, pepper and salt. Stir until smooth. Brown paste. Slowly add tomatoes and sugar. Let mixture boil. Remove from heat and serve. If too thick, add a little hot water and reheat.

Mary Morgan, McLain & Macey Love

QUICHE

4 slices bacon
3 eggs
½ cup biscuit mix
⅓ cup melted butter or oleo
1 ¼ cup milk
⅛ tsp. salt
2 cups shredded Swiss cheese
Dash of pepper

Lauren N. Doby - Granddaughter

Fry bacon until crisp, drain and crumble. Beat eggs, biscuit mix, butter or oleo, milk, salt and pepper until smooth. Pour into 9-inch pan or bigger pie plate or oblong baking dish. Sprinkle bacon and cheese over top and press gently. Bake at 350 degrees for 35 to 40 minutes.

Maudie Massey

ONION OMELET

2 T. butter
½ cup chopped onion
4 eggs
2 T. hot water
¼ tsp. salt
⅛ tsp. pepper

Fry the onion until tender in the butter. Separate the eggs. Beat the whites until stiff and the yolks until lemon color. Add the season and water to the yolks. Stir in the onion, fold into the whites, pour into frying pan that the onions were cooked in. Add a little more butter if necessary. Fry over low heat until brown on bottom. Fold over in half and serve.

BROWN GRAVY (1 QT)

½ cup vegetable oil
1 cup all purpose flour

Cook in skillet until brown in sauce pan. Add 1 qt. and 1 cup broth (either chicken, beef, turkey or whatever you have). Add salt and pepper to taste.

CREAMED OR MASHED POTATOES

5 lbs. white potatoes
½ lb. butter or oleo
1 teaspoon salt
1 heaping tablespoon mayonnaise
1 small can evaporated milk or
1 cup sweet milk

Wash and peel potatoes. Dice and boil until soft. Strain. Place in bowl and blend with potato masher adding butter, salt, mayonnaise and milk. Beat with electric mixer until smooth.

DEVILED EGGS

6 boiled eggs
2 T. hotdog relish
¼ tsp. salt
¼ tsp. pepper
1 tsp. sugar
1 tsp. grated onion (optional)
2 T. mayonnaise

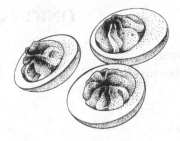

Peel boiled eggs and cut length-wise or cross-wise. Remove eggs yolks. Place in small bowl. Mash with fork until all lumps are gone. Add next six ingredients. Mix well with a teaspoon. Stuff egg whites with egg mixture.

QUICK MACARONI AND CHEESE

4 boxes macaroni and cheese

Boil macaroni until tender. Rinse in cold water to remove starch. Place in baking dish and stir in powdered cheese. Add 28 ounce or 1 lb. block cheddar cheese in separate dish. Beat 6 eggs, 1 quart milk, salt and pepper to taste. Pour on macaroni and cheese. Bake until milk congeals. Very good and cheesy.

BEST THING SINCE SANTA CLAUS
FRIED TURNIP ROOTS

Peel and wash fresh turnip roots. Slice about 1/4 inch thick. Set aside. Mix 1 cup corn meal and 1 cup all-purpose flour. Place turnip roots in 1 cup milk and 1 egg. Remove from milk mixture and place into corn meal and flour. Coat well. Cook in deep fryer until browned. May also be cooked in skillet. Brown one side then turn over and brown other side. Very good! If cooking only a few turnip roots then use less oil.

FRIED WHOLE OKRA

If using fresh okra, remove stem; frozen okra, leave as is. Cook like turnip roots, same ingredients.

ZUCCHINI SQUASH HUSH PUPPIES

Trim both ends of squash. Wash well. Grate 8 to 10 squash. Grate 3 or 4 medium onions into squash. Add 2 or 3 chopped green onions (optional). Add 2 eggs and enough corn meal and flour until thick enough to roll into small ball like hush puppies. Cook in deep fat until brown.

Steve Aycock (Pit Stop Mufflers) Mandy, Michael, Megan,
Tyson & Gage

Ms. Earline Broomfield & her white boy friend Dickie Dixon
(see Dickie and wife Donna on p. 38)

MEAT
MAIN DISHES

FRIED CHICKEN LIVERS

Remove small fatty part from livers. Wash chicken livers in baking soda and water (this will remove the bitter taste from livers and will not pop as much). Mix 1 egg, 1 cup milk. Put chicken livers in milk. Remove livers and place in self rising flour. Season with garlic salt and black pepper. Fry in deep cooking oil.

FRIED CHICKEN GIZZARDS

Wash and boil chicken gizzards 40 minutes. Seasoned with meat tenderizer and pepper. Remove from water and let cool. Emerge in milk and egg. Fry the same as livers.

EARLINE'S CHICKEN POT PIE
(25 PEOPLE)

1 gallon mix vegetables (chunky), drained
2 sticks or ½ pound oleo
½ cup flour
1 tsp. salt
½ tsp. black pepper
1 large can cream of chicken soup
10 chicken breasts, cooked and deboned
3 cups broth from chicken

Mix all ingredients together and pour into large baking dish. Top with pastry. Bake in a 350 degree oven until crust is golden brown for about 45 minutes or 1 hour.

Don't let your left hand know what your right hand doeth

PIE CRUST FOR CHICKEN POT PIE
AND ALL COBBLER PIES

3 ½ cups all purpose flour
1 ½ cups shortening
½ tsp. salt

Mix together until it resembles corn meal and add enough ice water to form a biscuit like dough. Roll out to desired thickness. Cover entire pie. Bake in oven at 350° for 30-45 minutes or until golden brown.

FAMILY SIZE CHICKEN & DRESSING

1 hen or chicken parts
½ gallon day old cornbread (or older)
½ loaf stale white bread
1 box Cornbread Stove Top Stuffing Mix
1 cup chopped celery
1 cup chopped onions
1 cup chopped bell pepper
1 small can cream of chicken soup
1 tsp. baking powder
10 eggs
½ lb. margarine

Davey

My 3 sons

Saute celery, onions and bell peppers together. Boil 1 hen or chicken parts in enough water to make broth for your dressing needs. Cook until tender. Mix together ½ gallon old cornbread, ½ loaf stale white bread, 1 box Stove Top Cornbread Stuffing Mix (both packs) and 1 tsp. baking powder. Add cooked celery, onion and bell peppers, 1 small can cream of chicken soup and 4 drops yellow food coloring. Add 10 eggs and mix all together with enough chicken broth to resemble uncooked cornbread. Pour all into baking pan and cook about 30 minutes in 400 degree oven. Stir around edges to mix with center dressing. Cook until done but not stiff. Remember, dressing becomes stiff after it sets awhile. Just add more chicken broth, do not stir or cook. Perfect every time.

Earline Broomfield

CROCK POT CHICKEN

1 small can cream of chicken soup
1 small can cream of celery soup
1 small can cream of mushroom soup
4 large chicken breasts
½ cup diced celery
½ cup minute rice

Jimmy Gibbs, Hugh Haralson,
Skipper Warren

Mix in crock pot the three can soups. Place the chicken on top of mixture and add the diced celery. Cook for 3 hours on high or 4 hours on low. Makes 4 servings. More rice, about ½ cup, and 2 additional chicken breasts may be added to make 6 servings.

Tillie Nack

AUNT DORA'S FRICASSEE CHICKEN

1 hen cut up
2 T. salt
½ cup vegetable oil
1 large onion, chopped
1 ½ cup celery, chopped
2 bay leaves
3 T. all purpose flour
Water

Place cut up chicken in hot vegetable oil and brown on all sides. Place chicken in stainless steel pot or any heavy pot. Add all ingredients at once, cover with water and simmer until done. To thicken, mix flour with cold water and pour over simmering chicken. Serve over hot biscuits or rice. Great eating.

DORITO CHICKEN CASSEROLE

1 chicken, cooked and deboned, diced*
1 bag Nacho Cheese Doritos
1 cup grated cheese
1 can cream of chicken soup
1 can of mushroom soup
½ can Ro Tel
½ onion, chopped

Randy Harvey

Layer chicken, Doritos, cheese and onion. Mix soups, milk and tomatoes. Pour over casserole and top with cheese. Bake at 375 degrees for 30 minutes. *One pound of ground beef may be substituted for chicken.

Gladis Pace

GOOD AND EASY CHICKEN

1 chicken cut up for frying
¼ cup flour
1 tsp. salt
½ tsp. pepper
2 tsp. dry mustard
1 tsp. paprika

Mix together flour, salt, pepper, dry mustard and paprika. Put in bag the flour mixture and chicken pieces. Shake to coat chicken pieces. Have oven preheated to 350 degrees and melt 3 T. butter in baking pan. Lay chicken in butter and turn once. Dot chicken generously with butter and bake uncovered for 40 minutes. Turn chicken once during this time. Then turn oven to 450 degrees and bake 10 to 15 minutes longer or until golden brown.

TURKEY OR CHICKEN AND DRESSING
(SERVES 25 PEOPLE)

This dressing may be made with frying size chicken breast, hen, or turkey, or turkey parts.

Boil meat until done adding enough water to make broth for the dressing.
1 9x12 inch pan cornbread
1/2 loaf white bread or 10 cooked biscuits may be used
Set aside.

Chop 1 stalk clean washed celery
Chop 2 cups onion
Chop 2 bell peppers

Place celery, bell pepper and onion, 1 pound margarine, 1 cup chicken broth in sauce pan. Cook until tender.

Add together cornbread, white bread, 1 box cornbread Stove Top Stuffing Mix (both packs), 1 can cream of chicken soup, bell pepper, onion and celery mixture, salt and pepper to taste. Add 12 whole eggs and add enough chicken broth to make look like cornbread mixture. Bake in large pan. Let bake about 30 minutes at 350 degrees. Stir well once. Place meat on top of the dressing. Cook until chicken is brown.

NO FAIL CHICKEN & DUMPLINGS
(20 SERVINGS)

In 1 gallon of water cook 20 chicken breasts, salt and pepper to taste. Save chicken broth and add 1 can cream of chicken soup. When done remove chicken and set aside. When chicken breasts cool, remove skin and debone.

In large pan add 5 cups all purpose flour, ¼ cup shortening, 1 tsp. baking powder, 1 tsp. salt, 5 eggs and 1 ¼ cups water.

Mix first 4 ingredients together until it looks like corn meal. Mix eggs and water. Beat until it turns yellow (do not over beat). Add to flour mixture, stirring until all comes together. With hands form dough to resemble biscuit dough. On floured board roll out small portions very thin. Cut in about 2 inch squares and drop into boiling chicken broth and cream of chicken soup. Add 1 stick butter or margarine. Drop quickly one dumpling at a time until all is used up. When last dumpling is in broth, boil about 5 minutes. (I add a few drops of yellow food coloring for a pretty color.)

CHICKEN CASSEROLE

Mix together:
2 cups cooked chicken, diced
1 can cream of mushroom soup
1 cup chopped celery
1 cup chopped green onion
3 hard cooked eggs, cut in small pieces
1 can of mushrooms
¼ cup almonds
½ cup salad dressing (mayonnaise)
2 cups cooked rice

Place in shallow baking dish. Top with 2 cups crushed potato chips. Bake at 350 degrees for 1 hour. Serves 6.

Tillie Nack

EARLINE'S FRIED CHICKEN

Wash chicken. Place in container and cover chicken in buttermilk. Refrigerate over night. Deep fry chicken in seasoned self rising flour with black pepper and garlic salt. Roll chicken in flour mixture. Cook until golden about 14 minutes and chicken comes to top of oil. This chicken may be cooked in your regular skillet. Juicy every time.

BAKED CHICKEN

Place desired chicken pieces in baking dish. Sprinkle with salt and pepper to taste. Cook uncovered until tender. Chicken will be light brown. Remove broth from chicken for gravy. Brown enough roux for thickening: 1 can of cream of chicken soup, broth from chicken, 1 can of water. Mix together and pour over chicken. Simmer in oven for 15 minutes.

BAKED HAM (WHOLE OR HALF)

Remove skin from ham and place in large pot and cover completely in cold water. Boil ham about 30 minutes. This will remove most of the salt. Remove ham from water. While warm, rub ham with light brown sugar. Place sliced pineapple all over ham by sticking toothpicks through pineapple to hold them in place. Put ham into baking bag with pineapple juice. Bake the half ham about 1 hour at 300 degrees; bake the whole ham 1 hour 45 minutes in a 300 degree oven. Don't forget to cut small slits into the baking bag to let out steam.

BAKED PORK CHOPS

Place pork chops in baking pan. Sprinkle with garlic salt, meat tenderizer and black pepper. Cook in oven at 350 degrees, turning over once. Cook until tender.

QUICK HAM BAKE - DAVEY'S STYLE

Have meat cutter to slice ham to desired thickness, about 1/4 inch thick. Rinse ham in cold water to remove bone particles. Place ham in roasting pan or any other pan. Place pineapple slices over ham, sprinkle with brown sugar. Add pineapple juice and bake in oven at 350 degrees uncovered, until tender about 30 minutes. Very good and juicy.

BBQ RIBS
(ANY AMOUNT)

Trim off excess fat and part of the lean meat on bottom edge of pork spare ribs. Wash. Sprinkle ribs with meat tenderizer, garlic salt and Lawry's Seasoned Salt. Put in plastic bag and place in refrigerator over night or pack bag in ice over night. Heat grill with charcoal until coals turn white. Put ribs on grill with inside of ribs turned  down. Turn ribs over often until tender. Country style ribs may be cooked the same way. If oven cooking, prepare ribs the same way and sprinkle with liquid smoke for a smoke flavor.

TENDER FRIED BEEF LIVER

Select already sliced beef liver. With sharp pointed knife remove white gristle like tissues. Rinse liver in cold water. Salt and pepper to taste. Mix together part flour and equal part corn meal and sprinkle on both sides of liver. Fry in medium hot skillet with just enough oil to fry, about ⅓ cup. Cook one side about 3 minutes. Remove liver from skillet. Remove cooking oil. Do not wash skillet. Cut 1 or 2 onions in thin slices. Pour into hot skillet. Cover onion with ⅓ cup water. Cover and steam until tender and pour over liver and serve hot.

If you lay in a bed of thorns, you won't know
which one stuck you.

GRILLED PORK STEAK

Place pork steaks on heated grill. Sprinkle lightly with your favorite meat tenderizer and garlic salt. Cook until tender. Serve hot.

FRIED PORK CHOPS

10 pork chops, or any amount
2 cups self rising flour
½ tsp. black pepper
1 tsp. meat tenderizer
1 tsp. garlic salt
1 egg
1 cup milk
Deep fat fryer or deep frying pan
Vegetable oil

Wash pork chops. Mix together 1 egg and 1 cup milk. Place pork in egg milk. Sift together flour, pepper, meat tenderizer and garlic salt. Roll pork chops in flour mixture. Drop in deep oil. Cook on high heat until brown. Remove from grease.

HAMBURGER STEAK

3 lbs. ground beef
3 eggs
¼ cup milk
⅛ tsp. meat tenderizer (I use 1 pinch)
½ tsp. black pepper
½ tsp. garlic salt

Mix all ingredients together. Shape in form of steaks or large hamburger patties. Place in baking pan and cook in oven until done. Drain off excess fat. Serve with cooked onion slices.

CORN BEEF AND CABBAGE

Boil corn beef in its own seasoning, about 2 1/2 to 3 hours. When tender, remove from water and let cool. Slice very thin by cutting cross the grain of the meat. This makes meat easy to chew and very tender. (Young people should ask older people what it means to cut cross the grain of the meat)

2 medium cabbages, fresh. Select cabbage with green leaves. Remove the green leaves from cabbage head and cut in ⅛ inch strips. Wash in cold water until clean. Place green cabbage leaves in 4 cups boiling water, add ham strips, 1 stick oleo, 1 tsp. salt, ¼ tsp. black pepper, 1 T. sugar. Boil until half done. Cut rest of cabbage and add to half done green cabbage. Cook until tender. Serve with corn beef or your favorite meat.

PEPPER STEAK

3 lb. round steaks, sliced and cut into 1 inch strips
3 large onions
3 bell peppers
⅛ tsp. pepper
⅛ tsp. salt

Boil steak in pot with salt and pepper until tender. In separate pot, cut bell pepper and onion in about 1 inch strips and cook until tender. Remove juice from onion and pepper. Remove juice from steak and add juices together for gravy. Pour steak, onion and bell pepper together. Pour gravy over steak mixture and serve over rice.

Dyess Brothers

95

CHILI, DAVEY'S STYLE

2 lbs. ground beef
3 cans red kidney beans
3 cans stewed tomatoes
2 cans tomato paste
3 cups water
½ tsp. black pepper
1 tsp. chili powder
Salt to taste

Cook ground beef in skillet, stirring until it becomes crumbly. Drain off excess fat and pour ground beef into large pot. Add red kidney beans and mash beans and meat with potato masher, just enough to make chili thicken. Add all other ingredients and bring to a rolling boil. Stir often. Lower heat and let simmer about 15 minutes.

MRS. GRIMES' CHILE BEANS

1 lb. ground beef
1 18 oz. can tomato sauce
¼ cup chopped onion
1 bay leaf
¼ cup chopped green pepper
1 tsp. dried oregano leaves, crushed
1 16 oz. can tomato catsup
1 15 oz. can Mrs. Grimes Chili Style Beans in Chili gravy

In large skillet, brown ground beef, onion and green pepper until meat is browned and vegetables are tender. Drain off fat. Stir in tomatoes, beans with gravy, tomato sauce, bay leaf, and oregano. Bring to a boil. Reduce heat. Cover and simmer 30 minutes. To each serving add shredded cheese. Makes 5 ½ cups, about 4 servings.

Mary Ruth Farmer

SALMON CROQUETTES

2 cans of pink salmon
2 large chopped onions
6 eggs
¼ tsp. black pepper
2 heaping T. flour
2 heaping T. cornmeal

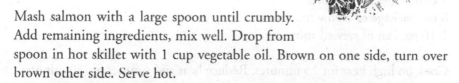

Mash salmon with a large spoon until crumbly.
Add remaining ingredients, mix well. Drop from
spoon in hot skillet with 1 cup vegetable oil. Brown on one side, turn over
brown other side. Serve hot.

COLD DAY VEGETABLE SOUP

5 lbs. stew beef
2 quarts water
2 bay leaves
2 cups of carrots, sliced
1 cup of chopped onion
1 cup of chopped celery
2 16 oz. can tomatoes
2 tsp. salt
½ tsp. pepper
1 tsp. sugar
½ tsp. thyme

Georgia Hunter, Ms. Earline Broomfield's Cousin

In large kettle or pot cover beef with water, add bay leaves. Let boil, reduce heat,
cover and simmer 2 hours or until meat is tender. Add rest of ingredients and heat
to boiling point. Reduce heat and let simmer about 20 minutes or until carrots are
tender.

Parents who eat sour grapes, put the children's teeth on edge.

LEFT OVER THANKSGIVING TURKEY SOUP

Place left over turkey bones and all in soup pot. Cover over completely with water. Boil turkey until all the meat leaves the bone. Remove bones from soup pot.

Add:
1 cup lima beans
1 cup whole kernel corn
8 oz. package of elbow macaroni
1 16 oz. can of stewed tomatoes

Cook on high heat for 15 minutes. Reduce heat and simmer for 30 minutes. Serve hot.

BAKED COON WITH POTATOES

Skin coon and place in salt and water overnight. Boil coon in fresh salt water and pepper, 1/2 cup vinegar until tender. Remove coon from water and place in baking dish. With back turn up, sprinkle lightly with garlic salt. Place 5 to 6 strips of uncooked bacon over coon. Peel and boil 6 to 8 small sweet potatoes in coon juice until half done. Place potatoes around coon and bake at 350° until bacon is brown and crisp and potatoes are tender.

RED BEANS & RICE

2 lbs. dry red beans
2 ham hocks or ham pieces (about 1 lb.)
1 medium onion cut up
2 quarts of water
Salt and pepper to taste

Add all ingredients together. Cook until beans are tender and juice is slightly thick. Serve over cooked rice.

MEAT LOAF (LARGE)

3 lbs. ground beef
1 lb. pork sausage
1 pkg. meat loaf seasoning
1 tsp. black pepper
1 tsp. salt
3 eggs
¼ cup milk

Mix all ingredients together. Put into loaf pan or shape as desired. Bake at 350 degrees about 1 hour. Slice and serve.

THE WILD SIDE - FRIED RABBIT

Cut rabbit into desired pieces. Place in pot and add 1 T. salt, ½ tsp. red pepper, ¼ cup vinegar. Cook until tender. Remove from pot and cover with enough buttermilk. Soak 5 or 10 minutes in buttermilk. Heat iron skillet with 1 cup vegetable oil. Remove rabbit from milk and cover in self rising flour. Fry until brown on both sides.

To make gravy, drain off vegetable oil and add 2 cups hot water and simmer until gravy thickens. Add more salt and black pepper if needed.

THE WILD - SQUIRREL STEW

Boil 3 squirrels in enough water to make stew. Add salt and black pepper to taste. Cook squirrel until tender.

Dumplings:
3 cups all purpose flour
1 tsp. baking powder
¼ cup shortening
2 eggs
1 ½ cups water

Mix 1½ cups tap water and 2 whole eggs together. Add to flour mixture to form biscuit like dough. Roll out on floured board until very thin. Cut dumplings in 2 inch squares. Add 1 stick oleo to boiling squirrel and juice. Drop dumplings one at a time. Let boil hard about 3 minutes. Cut heat down and simmer about 3 minutes. Serve hot.

Mike Gieger and Mark Ishee

100

OVEN CHICKEN & RICE

1 chicken in pieces
1 cup raw rice
1 pkg. onion soup mix
1 can cream of chicken soup
1 can water

Wash and dry chicken pieces. Lay in well oiled baking dish, skin up. Put rice around chicken. Mix together soup and water. Pour over chicken. Cover with foil. Bake at 350 degrees for two hours. Take off foil. Put under broiler just to brown.

Maudie Massey

CHICKEN POT PIE

Pastry for two crust pie:
½ cup chopped onion
6 T. butter
½ cup flour
3 cups chicken broth
3 cups cubed, cooked chicken
1 10 oz. pkg. frozen peas & carrots
½ cup chopped pimento

Raegan

Richie

Prepare pastry. Roll out on floured surface 1/4 inch thick. Cut to fit tops of individual casseroles. Place on ungreased baking sheet at 450° degrees for 10 to 12 minutes. In the meantime, cook onion in butter until tender but not brown. Blend in flour and 1 tsp. salt. Add broth all at once. Cook and stir until thick and bubbly. Pour into six heated individual casserole dishes. Place pastry on hot filling just before baking. Makes six servings. Note: Could be used in one large casserole dish.

Maudie Massey

MRS. BEE ELLIS
CHICKEN POT PIE
donated by daughters Pat and Maxie

1 whole fryer or 8 chicken breasts, cooked and de boned
1 - 1 lb. bag mixed vegetables, cooked

Place all in baking dish. Set aside.

In skillet add:
½ stick margarine
3 T. all-purpose flour
Make roux. Add 2 ½ cups chicken broth. Pour over vegetables &
chicken.

Crust:
You may use your own crust or use one of my crust recipes. Place over pie
and brown.

Sitting: Gina White ; Standing left to right: Marie White,
Eddie White, Joshua White, Cully White

DESSERTS
PIES

Miss USM Maggie Evans
of Bay Springs

SYL'S WHITE POTATO PIE

2 eggs
2 cups hot cooked mashed potatoes
½ cup margarine or butter, softened
¾ cup sugar
½ cup brown sugar
¼ cup evaporated milk
1 tsp. vanilla extract

Heat oven to 425 degrees. Prepare pastry, beat eggs slightly with hand beater. Beat in remaining ingredients. Pour half of potato mixture in one crust and remainder in the other. Bake 15 minutes. Reduce heat to 350 degrees. Bake until knife inserted in center comes out clean, about 45 minutes longer. Yields 2 pies, 8 servings each.

Maudie Massey

CHESS PIE

3 eggs
1 ½ T. flour
½ cup buttermilk
1 ½ cups sugar
1 stick butter, melted
1 tsp. vanilla

Mix all ingredients together. Pour in unbaked pie shell and bake at 350 degrees for 30 to 35 minutes.

Gladis Pace

❧

Misery loves company

APPLE PLATE PIE

5 tart apples
1 cup sugar
1 tsp. cinnamon
2 tsp. nutmeg
Pinch salt
2 T. all-purpose flour
4 T. butter
2-9 inch pie crust shells

Peel apples and slice thin. Place apples in a 9 inch pie crust shell. Mix together sugar, flour, cinnamon, nutmeg, salt and sprinkle over apples. Pat with butter. Place top crust over apples and seal top and bottom crust by pressing edges with a fork. Cut slits in top crust with a knife to let steam out. Sprinkle top crust with 2 tsp. sugar. Bake at 375 degrees until brown, about 1 hour 15 minutes.

MY MAMA'S PERFECT BLUEBERRY PIE

Line 9-inch pie plate with pie crust. Mix 4 cups blueberries with 1½ cups sugar, ½ tsp. nutmeg, 1 tsp. lemon juice, 3 T. all-purpose flour. Pour mixture in unbaked pie crust. Place top crust over berries. Seal edges and bake at 400 degrees for about 45 minutes or until golden brown. Serve warm or cold.

Earline Broomfield

NO CRUST COCONUT PIE

4 eggs
½ cup self-rising flour
½ stick margarine
1 tsp. lemon flavoring
1 ¾ cups sugar
2 cups milk
6 oz. can coconut

Mix all together and bake in 350 degree oven for 30-45 minutes.

Gladis Pace

FROZEN MOCHA CREAM PIE

CRUST:

2 cups reduced fat Oreo Cookie crumbs (about 20 cookies)
3 T. low fat margarine
4 oz. light cream cheese
5 oz. fat free cream cheese
1-14 oz. can sweetened condensed milk
1 ½ T. instant coffee dissolved in 1 T. hot water
1 tsp. vanilla
1 frozen fat free Cool Whip
⅔ cup fat free chocolate syrup

To make crust: In a small bowl, mix cookie crumbs and margarine. Set aside ¾ cup of mixture for later use as a topping. Press the remaining mixture into the bottom of a round 9-inch pie pan coated with non-stick cooking spray. Refrigerate 20 minutes to chill.

To make filling: In a large bowl, beat the cream cheese until smooth using an electric mixer on low to medium speed. Beat in condensed milk, chocolate syrup, coffee mixture and vanilla. Mix until smooth. Gently fold the frozen whipped topping into the filling and pour into prepared crust. Sprinkle the remaining crust mixture evenly over the top. Freeze for at least six hours until firm. Two-inch slice = 165 calories and 2 grams of fat.

Maudie Massey

CLINCH MOUNTAIN VINEGAR PIE

1 cup sugar

2 eggs

2 T. vinegar

2 T. flour/cornstarch

1 cup water

Small lump butter or margarine

1 tsp. lemon extract

Combine sugar, eggs, vinegar, flour (or corn starch), and water in double boiler and cook until thick and smooth, stirring constantly. Just before removing from heat stir in small lump of butter and some lemon extract. Pour into baked pie shell. If desired, the pie may be topped with frosting or whipped cream.

PECAN PIE

4 sticks oleo

1 cup sugar

4 cups white corn syrup

12 eggs

2 T. vanilla flavoring

4 cups pecan pieces

4 unbaked deep dish pie shells

Cream butter and sugar. Add corn syrup. Mix well. Add eggs and vanilla flavor and pecans, mixing well with spoon. Do not beat. Pour in unbaked pie shell and bake at 350 degrees until done, about 1 hour and 15 minutes. Makes 4 perfect pecan pies every time. During holiday season add two tablespoons Bacardi Rum for holiday touch.

FRIED COMBINATION PIE

2 -12 oz. bags dried apples
2 -12 oz. bags dried peaches
3 cups sugar
2 T. all-purpose flour
1 ½ stick margarine
3 cans 10-count biscuits
1 tsp. nutmeg
2 cups water

Cook apples separate. Peaches take longer to become tender. When done add together and mash and mix. Add next five ingredients. Mix well. Roll out biscuit about the size of a saucer. Place 1 heaping tablespoon of pie mix on dough. Fold over and press edges together with fork. Fry in ¼ cup oil or bake in oven. If frying, brown one side at a time.

Fried apple pies and peach pies are made the same way. Do not mix together.

FRIED SWEET POTATO PIES

4 cups cooked mashed sweet potatoes
1 tsp. vanilla
1 tsp. nutmeg
2 cups sugar
1 stick oleo
3 eggs
Biscuit or pie dough

Boil and mash potatoes. Add remaining ingredients. Roll dough thin and cut in circles about the size of a saucer. Fill half of the circle with potato mixture. Fold over, using a fork crimp edge together. Fry in cooking oil. When brown turn over and brown other side. Drain on paper towels.

LEMON MERINGUE PIE

1 ½ cups sugar
⅓ cup corn starch
½ cup water
3 egg yolks slightly beaten
3 T. butter or margarine
2 tsp. grated lemon peel
½ cup lemon juice
2 drops yellow food coloring

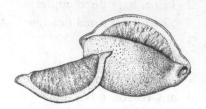

Prepare 9-inch baked pie shell. Mix sugar and corn starch. Gradually stir in water. Cook over medium heat stirring constantly until mixture thickens and boils. Gradually stir at least half the hot mixture into egg yolk. Blend into hot mixture in pan. Boil and stir 1 minute. Remove from heat and stir in butter, lemon peel, juice and food coloring. Pour into baked pie shell. Prepare meringue and spread over pie.

MERINGUE

Beat 3 egg whites until foamy stiff. Add 6 T. sugar, 1 T. at a time. Beat until stiff and glossy. Beat in 1/2 tsp. vanilla, 1/2 tsp. cream of tartar. Spread over entire pie. Bake about 10 minutes or until golden brown.

MY FAVORITE PIE

10 medium size sweet potatoes
½ lb. butter or margarine
3 cups sugar
1 tsp. nutmeg
2 T. vanilla flavor
12 eggs
1 T. Bacardi rum (optional)
1 small can condensed milk
4 - 9 inch deep dish pie shells

Boil potatoes in hull until done. Cool with cold water and peel. Place butter in cooked potatoes. Mash with potato masher. Add next ingredients until all are mixed well. Beat with mixer about 2 minutes. Pour into 4 - 9 inch deep dish uncooked pie shells. Place in 350 degree oven until done, approximately 1 hour 20 minutes.

ANNIE LEE'S EGG PIE

1 cup sugar
1 T. all-purpose flour
3 eggs
1-8 oz. glass of milk
1 tsp. vanilla
Nutmeg
1/2 stick oleo

Cream sugar and oleo. Add flour. Beat in eggs, milk and flavor. Pour in unbaked deep-dish pie crust. Sprinkle with nutmeg. Bake in a 350 degree oven about 45 minutes and the pie is not shaky.

Larry Gressett & Ashley Gressett

FRESH BLUEBERRY PIE

3 cups fresh blueberries or huckleberries

1 ½ cups sugar

½ stick oleo

2 heaping T. all-purpose flour

1 tsp. nutmeg

1 tsp. vanilla flavor

1 unbaked 2-crust pie shell

In saucepan, mix all ingredients together. Cook over low heat until butter melts and sugar dissolves. Pour in unbaked deep dish pie shell. Cover with remaining pie crust. Cut slits in top crust. Bake at 350 degrees approximately 1 hour until crust is golden brown. Cool before cutting.

BUTTERMILK PIE

3 eggs

1 cup buttermilk

1 heaping T. flour

1 stick butter or margarine

1 cup sugar

1 tsp. vanilla

½ tsp. nutmeg

Cream sugar and butter. Add eggs, flour and buttermilk. Fold in vanilla and nutmeg. Pour into unbaked pie shell. Bake at 350 degree oven until pie is firm but not stiff, about 45 minutes.

THIRON & MARTHA SIMMONS
RHUBARB PIE

2 cups chopped rhubarb
1 cup sugar
1 cup strawberries
1 egg
2 T. all purpose flour

Mix all together, pour into unbaked pie shell. Cook 45 minutes at 350 degrees.

Theron M. & Martha L. Simmons

Mike Thames & Craig Byrd, PECO Foods, Inc.

FRESH PEACH PIE

1 unbaked 2 - crust pie shells
5 cups fresh peaches
1 ½ tsp. lemon juice
1 ½ cups sugar
¼ cup all-purpose flour
¼ tsp. nutmeg
1 stick oleo

Mix peaches and lemon juice. Stir together rest of the ingredients. Mix well. Pour into piecrust. Dot with oleo. Cover with other crust. Put small slits in the top crust. Bake about 1 hour at 400 degrees.

PERFECT MERINGUE #1

2 egg whites
3 T. sifted powdered sugar
1 pinch salt
6 drops vanilla flavor

Put the egg whites in a bowl and beat until stiff. Sift the sugar and salt. Add the flavoring and continue beating until the mixture looks glossy. Pile on top of the pie with a large spoon. Place in a fairly warm oven about 325 degrees. Bake for 10-12 minutes. The top will be slightly golden brown.

MAMA'S RICE PUDDING

3 cups cooked rice
1 cup sugar + ½ cup raisins (optional)
2 cups milk
1 stick oleo
1 tsp. vanilla
3 eggs, beaten

Mix all together. Pour over cooked rice and bake in a 350 degree oven about 1 hour or until it congeals.

BIG BANANA PUDDING

10 bananas

2 -12 oz. bags vanilla wafers

½ gal. milk

6 egg yolks

2 ½ cups sugar

2 T. vanilla flavor

4 drops yellow food coloring

¾ cup all-purpose flour

In double boiler mix sugar and flour together. Mix well so it will not lump when adding milk. Add milk, mixing well. Cook in double boiler over boiling water until it thickens. Remove from heat. Beat in egg yolks all at once, then add flavor and food coloring. Pour wafers in large serving bowl. Peel bananas, slice crosswise over wafers. Pour pudding over wafers and bananas. Serve warm or cold.

BREAD PUDDING

8 slices toasted white bread

4 eggs

1 tsp. vanilla flavor

½ tsp. nutmeg

2 cups sugar

3 cups sweet milk

1 ½ sticks melted butter

Cut bread in four to six pieces. Toss in melted butter. Beat eggs and add all ingredients. Pour over bread and bake in 350 degree oven until done, about 1 hour or until it congeals.

CUSTARD BREAD PUDDING

2 eggs
2 cups milk
1 cup sugar
1 T. butter or margarine, melted
1 tsp. ground cinnamon
10 slices day-old bread (crusts removed), cut into ½ inch cubes
1 cup raisins

Sauce:
⅔ cup sugar
2 T. all-purpose flour
1 cup water
7 T. butter or margarine
1 tsp. vanilla extract

In large bowl, combine eggs, milk, sugar, butter and cinnamon. Add the bread cubes and raisins and mix well. Pour into a greased 11x7x2 inch-baking dish. Bake at 350 degrees until a knife inserted near the center comes out clean. For the sauce, combine sugar in a small pan with flour and water until smooth. Add butter. Bring to a boil over medium heat, cook and stir for 2 minutes. Remove from heat and stir in vanilla. Serve warm or cold over pudding. Yields 8 servings.

Maudie Massey

Scarlett and Lexi Kirkland

MAMA & MINE BISCUIT PUDDING

10 biscuits (I prefer canned biscuits)
2 cups sugar
6 eggs
2 T. vanilla flavor
1 tsp. nutmeg
1 qt. + 1 cup milk
1 stick oleo or butter
few drops yellow food coloring

My mother - Lela Edison

Bake biscuits until done. You may use your own left over homemade biscuits. Split biscuits in halves and place in pan with inside of biscuit facing up. Brown lightly. In mixing bowl, mix eggs and sugar together with electric mixer. Add milk, nutmeg, flavor and food coloring. With biscuits facing up, pour liquid mixture over biscuits and dot with butter or oleo. Let set for 15 minutes so biscuits can soak. Place in a 350 degree oven for about 30 minutes or until eggs and milk congeal. Do not over cook.

ALL COBBLERS PIE CRUST

3 cups all-purpose flour
1 ½ cups shortening
1 tsp. salt
¾ cup ice cold water

Mix flour, salt and shortening together until they resemble coarse cornmeal. Add ice water, stirring until well blended. Roll in flour until it looks like biscuit dough. Place ¼ of dough on floured board. Roll out thin and cover entire pie. Bake at 350 degrees.

Tongue and teeth fall out sometimes

EASY COBBLER

1 cup all-purpose flour
1 stick oleo
1 tsp. baking powder
1 cup milk
1 cup sugar
1 large can fruit
(for larger cobbler, double the ingredients)

Heat oven to 400 degrees. Place oleo into desired pan and melt in oven. Mix flour, sugar, baking powder and milk together. Pour on top of oleo. Heat fruit in saucepan. Pour on top of batter. Bake until brown about 45 minutes.

FRESH PEAR COBBLER

4 cups sliced pears
3 cups sugar
1½ sticks oleo
1 T. vanilla flavor
½ tsp. nutmeg
2 T. all-purpose flour
6 cups of water
1 unbaked pie crust

Boil four cups sliced pears in 6 cups water until tender. Pour in baking pan large enough to hold all ingredients. Add oleo and vanilla. Mix together sugar, nutmeg, and flour. Sprinkle over pears. Cover with pie crust. Bake at 350 degrees until crust is golden brown for 1 hour.

Steve Dixon

SWEET POTATO COBBLER

6 medium sweet potatoes
½ lb. margarine
3 cups sugar and 2 heaping T. plain flour
1 tsp. nutmeg
2 T. vanilla flavor
1 unbaked pie shell

Slice potatoes about ¼ inch thick. Boil in 4 cups of water until tender. Drain potatoes and pour in a baking pan. Mix together sugar, flour, nutmeg and liquid from the potatoes. Pour over cooked potatoes. Dot with butter and vanilla flavor. Roll out pie crust. Cover entire pie. Bake at 350 degrees until crust is golden brown and juice is slightly thick.

FRESH BLUEBERRY COBBLER

3 cups blueberries
1½ sticks oleo
3 cups sugar
2 T. all-purpose flour
1 tsp. nutmeg
1 tsp. vanilla flavor
1 cup water
1 unbaked pie shell

In baking dish, add uncooked blueberries and oleo. Mix together flour, sugar, and nutmeg. Pour over berries. Add vanilla flavor and water. Cover top with your favorite pie crust in a 350 degree oven. Cook until crust is golden brown and juice is slightly thick.

Mary Morgan, McLain, & Macy Love

CHEDDAR APPLE PIZZA

Pastry for a single-crust pie
4 large baking apples, peeled and cut into ¼ inch slices
  (about 5 cups)
½ cup shredded cheddar, mozzarella or swiss cheese
½ cup packed brown sugar
½ cup chopped walnuts
½ tsp. ground cinnamon
½ tsp. ground nutmeg
2 T. cold butter or margarine

Roll pastry to fit a greased 12 inch pizza pan; flute edges. Bake at 400 degrees for 10 minutes. Arrange apples in a single layer in a circular pattern to completely cover the pastry. Sprinkle with cheese. Combine brown sugar, walnuts, cinnamon, nutmeg and sprinkle over cheese. Cut butter into small pieces and dot top of pizza. Bake for 20 minutes or until apples are tender. Cut into wedges. Serve warm. Yields 12 servings.

Maudie Massey
Freeport, Illinois

EARLINE'S VANILLA HOMEMADE ICE CREAM

10 eggs
1 cup sugar
1 qt. sweet milk
1 can sweetened condensed milk
1 can evaporated milk
2 tsp. vanilla flavor

In a large mixing bowl beat 10 egg yolks. Save egg whites in another bowl. Add sugar and beat. Heat sweet milk until hot. Do not boil. Add condensed milk to heated milk. Add evaporated milk and flavor. Beat egg whites until stiff. Stir egg whites into ice cream mixture. Pour into electric freezer or hand frozen. Turn until freezer stops turning.

STRAWBERRY DELIGHT

Pound Cake (loaf pan size, homemade
or store bought)
1 small pkg. strawberry Jell-O
1 small pkg. instant vanilla pudding
1 pt. strawberries, sliced
1 small carton Cool Whip
2 to 3 whole strawberries for garnish

Break pound cake into bite-sized pieces and arrange on the bottom
of a square pan or dish. Prepare Jell-O as directed on package and
pour over cake pieces. Chill until set.

Prepare pudding as directed and spoon over jello. Arrange sliced
strawberries over pudding. Cover with Cool Whip and use 2 to 3
whole strawberries for garnish, if desired.

Gladis Pace

Richard Headrick & Ms. Earline

DR. VERONICA JACKSON JOHNSON
SWEET POTATO PIE WITH COCONUT

2 large sweet potatoes
1½ cup sugar
1 stick of butter or oleo
½ tsp. nutmeg
¼ tsp. cinnamon
1 T. vanilla flavor
4 oz. bakers coconut
¼ cup evaporated milk

Glenn A. Johnson

Boil potatoes in skins until tender. Add butter, mix well. Add all other ingredients. Mix until all lumps are gone. Stir in coconut. Pour in unbaked pie crust. Cook at 350 degrees until done for about 1 hr 15 mins.

EARLINE'S CHOCOLATE PIE

1½ cup sugar
2 T. cocoa
½ cup flour
½ cup milk
½ cup evaporated milk
3 egg yolks (save egg whites for topping)
½ stick of oleo

Mix well with wire whisk. Cook over direct heat until thick and bubbly. This will become thick quickly. Beat with wire whisk until smooth. Pour into cooked pie shell. Top with meringue and brown at 350 degrees.

RICE PUDDING

3 cups cooked rice
½ stick of butter or margarine
1 cup raisins
½ tsp. nutmeg
3 eggs well beaten
½ cup milk
1½ cup sugar

Mix together. Bake at 350 degrees for 30 mins or until golden brown.

BRELAND GREEN, THE BANJO MAN, FRESH STRAWBERRY PIE

1 ½ cup sugar
1 ½ cup water
¼ cup cornstarch
1 3 oz. box strawberry Jell-O
1 qt fresh strawberries
2 pastry shells, baked
Cool whip

Combine sugar, water, and cornstarch. Cook about 10 minutes or until thick and clear. Remove from heat and add Jell-O. Put in refrigerator for 3 ½ hours. Wash and slice fresh strawberries. Add to Jell-O mixture. Pour into brown pie crusts. Top with Cool Whip.

EARLINE'S COCONUT PIE

1 cup sugar
½ cup all-purpose flour
2 cups milk
½ stick margarine
3 egg yolks, save egg white for topping
1 tsp. vanilla
1 oz. can Baker's coconut (save 1 T. for top)
1 baked pie shell

Mix first 2 ingredients well. Add milk and margarine and egg yolk. I use a wire whisk. Pour in double boiler. Cook until thick. Add coconut and vanilla flavor. Pour into baked pie shell.

Topping:

3 egg whites

Beat with electric mixer until it stays in a pan when turned upside down. Add ½ cup sugar, ½ teaspoon cream of tartar and ½ teaspoon vanilla flavor. Mix with spoon. Pour on top of pie. Sprinkle with tablespoon coconut. Brown in oven about 400 degrees.

PERFECT MERINGUE 2

3 egg whites
1/8 tsp. salt
1/4 tsp. cream of tartar
6 T. sugar
1 tsp. vanilla extract

Beat egg whites, salt, and cream of tartar until they begin to stiffen. Beat in sugar 1 T. at a time. Add vanilla. Continue beating until meringue stands in stiff peaks. Spread on pie. Brown in 400 degree oven 5 to 8 minutes.

EARLINE'S CHOCOLATE PIE 2
(Makes 2 Pies)

3 cups sugar
3/4 cup flour
4 T. Hershey's Cocoa
2 cups milk
1 cup evaporated milk
1/2 stick margarine
6 egg yolks (save egg whites for topping)
2 baked pie shells

Mix first three ingredients well. Add milk, margarine, and egg yolks. Mix with wire whisk. In copper bottom or stainless pot, cook over direct heat until thick and creamy. Stir constantly as this will thicken quickly. Pour into two baked pie shells.

Topping:

Beat egg whites until stiff. Add 1 cup of sugar, 1 teaspoon of tartar, 1 teaspoon of vanilla flavor. Mix with spoon. Pour on top of pie. Bake in oven at 350 degrees about 15 minutes or until brown.

CHARLES HOLDER
KEY LIME PIE

1 can Eagle Brand condensed milk
3 egg yolks
½ cup key lime juice
1 graham cracker pie crust

I make my own pie crust with vanilla wafers. For a bigger thick pie, double the recipe.

Place milk in a bowl or pan. Add egg yolks. Mix well. Stir in lime juice. When thick, pour into pie crust. Place in refrigerator until set and ready to serve.

CHOCOLATE CREAM PIE

1 ½ cups sugar
⅓ cup all-purpose flour
2 T. baking cocoa
½ tsp. salt
1 ½ cups water
1 can (12 Oz.) evaporated milk
5 egg yolks, beaten
½ cup butter or margarine
1 tsp. vanilla extract
Whipped topping

Jasper County Sheriff
Kenneth Cross

In a large saucepan, combine the first six ingredients until smooth. Cook and stir over medium-high heat until thickened and bubbly, about 2 minutes. Reduce heat, cook and stir minutes longer. Remove from heat. Stir 1 cup hot mixture into egg yolks. Return all to the pan; bring to a gentle boil, stirring constantly. Remove from heat and stir in butter and vanilla. Cool slightly. Pour warm filling into pastry shell. Cool for 1 hour. Refrigerate until set. Just before serving garnish with whipped topping. Yield 6-8 servings.

Maudie Massey

Steve Aycock (Pit Stop Mufflers) Mandy
Michael, Megan, Tyson, & Gage

CAKES
COOKIES

To
Earline
God Bless!
Bob Saxton
10-5-07

Bob Saxton

PIXY POUND CAKE

1 cup vegetable shortening (Crisco)
1/2 cup butter
3 cups sugar
6 eggs
3-1/4 cups flour
1 level tsp. baking powder
1/2 tsp. vanilla flavoring
1/2 tsp. lemon flavoring

Cream shortening, butter, and sugar well. Add eggs one at a time. Sift flour, baking powder, and salt. Add to mixture alternately with milk. Add flavorings. Beat thoroughly. Bake in 10 inch tube pan 1-1/2 hours at 350 degrees. Do not look at cake for first hour.

When cake is done pour this syrup slowly over cake:

3 T. butter
1 cup sugar
1/2 tsp. lemon juice with enough water to make 1/2 cup
2 tsp. grated lemon zest

Melt butter in sauce pot. Add remaining ingredients. Cook until sugar is dissolved. Cool cake in pan.

Mrs. Jimmie Robinson

Cooper McMullian

129

JULIA WELBURN'S FAVORITE CAKE

2 cups all purpose flour
½ cup cocoa
½ cup shortening
3 cups sugar
2 sticks oleo margarine
5 eggs
1 ¼ cup sweet milk
½ tsp. baking powder
1 tsp. vanilla

Cream sugar and shortening, oleo together. Add all other ingredients. Bake in tube pan for 1 ½ hours at 350 degrees.

ICING

2 cups sugar
½ cup cocoa
⅔ cup sweet milk
¼ tsp. salt
1 stick oleo
1 tsp. vanilla

Bring all ingredients to a boiling point. Punch holes in cake with pencil. Pour icing over hot cake.

LEMON ICING

3 T. cornstarch
½ cup cold water
1 egg slightly beaten
½ cup sugar
¼ tsp. salt
Grated rind and juice of 1 lemon

Mix cornstarch and water into smooth paste. Combine eggs, sugar, salt, lemon rind and juice. Gradually add boiling water to cornstarch. Cook and stir over low flame until mixture thickens. Cool and spread over layers.

COCOA APPLE CAKE

3 eggs
2 cups granulated sugar
1 cup (2 sticks) margarine
½ cup water
2 ½ cups all purpose flour
2 T cocoa
1 tsp. baking soda
1 tsp. cinnamon
1 tsp. allspice
1 cup finely chopped nuts
½ cup chocolate bits
2 apples cored and grated or finely chopped (2 cups)
1 tsp. vanilla

Jasper County Sheriff
Deputy Douglas Wheaton

Beat together eggs, sugar, margarine and water until fluffy. Sift flour, cocoa, soda, cinnamon and allspice. Add to creamed mixture and mix well. Fold in nuts, chocolate, apples and vanilla until evenly distributed. Spoon into greased and floured 10-inch loose bottom tubed pan. Bake in 325 degree oven 60-70 minutes until cake tests done. Makes one cake. Serves 10.

CHERRY DUMP CAKE

16.4 oz. crushed pineapple spread over bottom of pan
16.5 oz. cherry pie filling spread over pineapple
1 yellow cake mix, sprinkle dry over cherries
2 sticks butter cut in patties, placed over cake mix
1 cup chopped walnuts, sprinkle over top

Bake in a 9" x 13" pan on 350 degrees for 50- 60 minutes.

Maudie Massey

A man is known by the company he keeps

BETTER THAN SEX CAKE

1 pkg. yellow cake mix
½ cup vegetable oil
1 large pkg. instant vanilla pudding mix
1 large can crushed pineapple (in own juice)
1-12 oz. cool whip

Mix cake according to directions. Bake in a sheet cake pan.

While cake cools, mix pineapple and sugar in sauce pan. Cook about 20 minutes or until syrupy. Pour on cake while HOT. Punch holes in cake with fork and COOL CAKE completely.

Mix pudding according to directions. Spread on cake. Top with Cool Whip. Refrigerate.

Eat and enjoy. This recipe was the winner in a bake off at our church! Now ain't that a kick in the teeth!

(copied)

LEMON ICEBOX CAKE

1 butter cake mix (Duncan Hines or yellow mix)
2 cans condensed milk
½ cup lemon juice
7 oz. Cool Whip

Bake butter cake mix according to directions on package into three layers. Mix the condensed milk and lemon juice. Fold in Cool Whip. Ice each layer and in between with the Cool Whip mixture (this makes a lot of frosting). Keep cake in the refrigerator.

Gladis Pace

COCONUT CAKE

1 cup butter
3 ½ cups flour
2 cups sugar
3 whole eggs
1 tsp. vanilla
1 ¾ cup milk
¼ tsp. salt
2 tsp. baking powder (heaping)
⅓ cup coconut milk

Cream butter, sugar and eggs, adding one at a time. Add 1 cup of flour and mix well using small amount of milk. Add other ingredients. Bake in a 350 degree oven for 30-40 minutes. Use 3 regular 8" round cake pans. Grease and flour pans well. Let cakes slightly cool. Stack with 7minute frosting. Use freshly ground coconut. Place over frosting.

7 MINUTE FROSTING

2 unbeaten egg whites
2 tsp. corn syrup
¼ tsp. cream of tartar
1 ½ cup granulated sugar
⅓ cup cold water
1 tsp. vanilla
Dash of salt

Mix together above ingredients over medium heat for 7 minutes, stirring constantly to avoid sticking. Spread on cake of choice.

BUTTER CREAM ICING

⅓ cup butter or margarine
3 cups confectioner's sugar
1 ½ tsp. vanilla
2 T. milk

Blend butter and sugar. Stir in vanilla and milk, Beat until smooth and of spreading consistency.

HOLIDAY POUND CAKE

1 cup butter (Land of Lake), salted
½ cup shortening
1 package 3 oz. cream cheese, softened
2 ½ cups sugar
5 eggs
3 cups cake flour
1 tsp. baking powder
½ tsp. salt
1 cup buttermilk
1 tsp. lemon extract
1 tsp. vanilla extract
Strawberry ice cream optional
Sliced fresh strawberries, optional

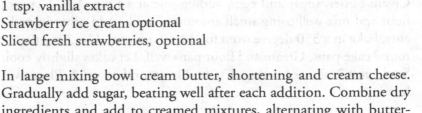

In large mixing bowl cream butter, shortening and cream cheese. Gradually add sugar, beating well after each addition. Combine dry ingredients and add to creamed mixtures, alternating with buttermilk. Stir in extracts and pour into a greased flour fluted tube pan. Bake at 325 degrees for 1 hour and 20 minutes or until toothpick inserted near the center comes out clean. Cool for ten minutes; remove from pan to wire rack. Serve with strawberries or serve with ice cream if desired. Yields 12-16 servings.

Maudie Massey

CREAM CHEESE FROSTING

1-8 oz. package cream cheese, softened
1 stick oleo or butter, softened
1 T milk
1 tsp. vanilla
¼ tsp. salt
3 ½ cups confectioner's sugar

Blend cheese, milk, vanilla, salt and butter. Add sugar, beating until creamy and ready to spread. Food color may be added for special occasion.

SUNDAY DINNER LEMON STACK CAKE

½ cup shortening
1 cup sugar
2 eggs
1½ cups cake flour
½ tsp. salt
1 tsp. lemon extract
½ cup milk
Lemon filling

Cream the shortening. Gradually work in the sugar, add the eggs, well beaten, and beat until the mixture is well blended. Sift the dry ingredients together and add alternately with the milk to the first mixture. Add the extract and beat and blend the mixture. Pour into two well-greased cake pans. Bake at 375 degrees for 20 minutes or until done. Spread with lemon filling and dust with powdered sugar.

MY MAMA'S LEMON FILLING

4 T. corn starch
½ cup cold water
¼ tsp. salt
1 egg slightly beaten
¾ cup sugar
1 ½ cup boiling water
Grated rind and juice of 1 lemon

Mix corn starch and water to form a paste. Combine the next 5 ingredients. Stir in the boiling water. Cook and stir until thick like jelly. Spread between the layers of cake and top.

Earline Broomfield

LEMONY CHEESE SQUARES

1 box yellow cake mix (may use lemon supreme)
¼ cup chopped pecans
1 stick margarine, melted
1 egg

Mix all the above ingredients and press into a 9x13 inch pan. Mix the following ingredients with a mixer:

8 oz. cream cheese (softened)
2 drops lemon extract
2 eggs
1 box confectioner's sugar

Pour this over cake mixture and bake at 350 degrees for 35 to 40 minutes. Serves 24.

Gladis Pace

OATMEAL COOKIES

½ cup butter or oleo
1 cup sugar
2 cups oatmeal
3 cups flour
4 T. milk
2 eggs
1 tsp. cinnamon
½ tsp. cloves
1 cup chopped raisins
1 cup chopped nuts (pecans)

Cream the butter and sugar together. Mix baking soda and milk. Add eggs into sugar mixture one at a time. Beat. Add milk, flour, oatmeal, spices and nuts. Drop by teaspoon on greased cookie sheet. Bake at 325 degrees about 15 minutes. Makes about 40 cookies.

Devin Mitchell

AUNT MARY'S TEACAKES

3 cups self rising flour
2 eggs and ¾ cup water mixed
2 tsp. lemon flavor
1 stick butter
2 ½ cups sugar

Make a small well in flour. Add all ingredients together. Pour into flour well. Work in with fingertips to form dough. Roll out and cut with cookie cutter. Bake until golden brown in a 350 degree oven.

Earline Broomfield

SUGAR COOKIES

½ cup butter or oleo
¼ cup shortening
1 cup sugar
2 eggs
1 tsp. vanilla
2 ½ cups all purpose flour
1 tsp. baking powder
1 tsp. salt

Mix thoroughly the sugar, eggs and vanilla. Blend in flour, baking powder and salt. Cover dough and chill at least 1 hour. Roll dough about ½ inch thick on lightly floured cloth covered board. Cut into desired shapes. Place on ungreased cookie sheet. Bake until light brown about 8 to 10 minutes.

Hawk Hendry

Sydney Stringer

MY FAVORITE MOLASSES COOKIES

1 stick margarine
1¼ T baking soda
1 cup molasses
½ cup buttermilk
4½ cups all purpose flour

2 cups sugar
½ cup Wesson Oil
1 egg
1 tsp. vanilla or ginger

Heat pot and pour in first four ingredients. Remove from heat immediately and set aside and let stand. Mix remaining ingredients all together well to form a dough. Pinch off in small balls and pat them out in your hand. Bake at 375 degree oven until brown.

Devin Mitchell

DAVEY'S 4TH GENERATION TEACAKES

½ cup butter
½ cup shortening
1½ cups sugar
3 eggs
4 cups all purpose flour
2 tsp. baking powder
1 tsp. baking soda
1 tsp. nutmeg
⅓ cup buttermilk

Cream sugar, butter and shortening together well. Add eggs and beat well. Add flavor. Mix baking powder, soda and flour together. Add milk. Mix all together to form a dough. Roll out ¼ inch thick and place on baking sheet. Sprinkle with sugar. Bake at 350 degrees until light brown. Makes 4 dozen.

Earline Broomfield

~

If a man brings a bone, he will take a bone.

OLD FASHIONED TEACAKES

1 cup shortening
2 cups sugar
2 eggs
1 tsp. nutmeg
5 ½ cups flour
1 cup buttermilk
1 tsp. vanilla

Cream shortening and sugar well. Add flour and buttermilk alternately to creamed mixture. Add nutmeg and vanilla. Roll out on lightly floured pastry board about ½ inch thick. Cut with cookie cutter and place on ungreased baking sheet. Bake in a 375 degree oven for 15 minutes. Makes about 3 ½ dozen teacakes.

Maudie Massey

APRICOT NECTAR CAKE

2 boxes Duncan Hines lemon supreme cake mix
8 eggs
½ cup sugar
1 cup vegetable oil
2 cups apricot nectar

In large mixing bowl combine cake mix and next four ingredients. Beat well with electric mixer. Pour in large sheet cake pan. Bake approximately 30 minutes at 300 degrees or until inserted toothpick comes out clean. This cake may be cut in half.

GLAZE

1 box confectioner's sugar
1/2 cup Lemon juice

Mix well. Pour and spread over cake while hot.

MISSISSIPPI'S BEST
THE GLENN PARKER CAKE (Big)

2 boxes Duncan Hines butter cake mix
1 cup vegetable oil
8 eggs
1 cup evaporated milk & 1 cup milk
2 cans coconut pecan icing

Mix according to package directions. Stir into the cake
2 cans of coconut pecan icing. Mix well. Pour in 2 well
greased, extra large cake pans. (May also be cooked in
sheet cake pans). Cook in 350 degree oven until cake is
done. Let cool.

ICING

1 8 Oz. block cream cheese
1 4 Oz. block cream cheese
1 stick margarine

1 1/2 boxes confectioners sugar
1 T vanilla flavoring

Mix well. Spread icing on first layer. Sprinkle first layer
with chopped pecans. Stack second layer on top. Ice top
and sides. Sprinkle top and sides with chopped pecans.

Earline Broomfield

Davey, Ms. Earline, Glenn and wife, Shirley

Glenn Parker Family

Parker & Deuce

April & Prince Arnold

Glenn & Shirley's son, Brian Parker

The Parker grandchildren
Parker, Deuce, & Isaiah

Glenn & Shirley's daughter, son-in-law, & family,
The Arnold Family

Shirley Parker

141

ELVIS PRESLEY CAKE

1 (18 ¼ ounce) box of yellow cake mix
1 (3 ounce) box of vanilla pudding (not instant)
4 eggs
½ cup oil
1 cup milk
1 (16 ounce) can crushed pineapple, undrained
1 cup sugar

Mix cake mix, pudding, eggs, oil and milk. Beat until smooth. Bake as directed on box. While cake is baking, boil pineapple and sugar on top of the stove until melted. While cake is hot, punch holes and pour pineapple mixture over it. Let cool.

FROSTING

1 (8 ounce) package cream cheese, softened
1 stick margarine, softened
3 cups of confectioners sugar
½ cup chopped pecans

Beat cream cheese and butter until smooth. Add confectioners sugar and beat until creamy. Add pecans. Mix well.

Tony Bolter & Jackie Dollar

MRS. WELBURN'S FAVORITE COCONUT CAKE

2 boxes Duncan Hines white cake mix
4 T. vegetable oil
2 ½ cups milk
6 eggs

Mix and cook cake by package directions. Remove 1 layer from pan while still warm. When done stick holes all over cake with toothpick so filling will go into cake.

FILLING

1 small can crushed pineapple
¾ cup sugar
½ cup water
1 stick margarine or oleo
I tsp. all purpose flour

Zach, Hannah Grace, John Paul
Children of Zachary & Amie

Cook over low heat, stirring until all is melted. Spoon filling over first layer while cake is warm. Add second layer.

ICING

3 egg whites
1 cup water
1 tsp. vanilla flavor
1 cup sugar
1 tsp. cream of tartar

Lana & Reagan Buckley
Children of Michael & Randi
Grandparents Ronnie & Carolyn Buckley

In sauce pan cook sugar and water until it looks like syrup and bubbly. Beat egg whites until stiff. While beating pour syrup over egg whites while hot. Mix well with spoon. Stir in cream of tartar and flavor. Spread over cake. Sprinkle with coconut.

HUMMINGBIRD CAKE

1 pkg. yellow cake mix
1 8 oz. can crushed pineapple, undrained
3 small bananas peeled and mashed, about 1 cup
½ cup water
½ cup vegetable oil
3 large eggs
1 tsp. vanilla extract
1 tsp. ground cinnamon

Preheat oven 350 degrees. Lightly grease and flour 2 - 9 inch round cake pans. Combine cake mix, pineapple with juice, mashed bananas, water, oil, vanilla extract and cinnamon in large bowl. Beat one minute with an electric mixer and bake until golden brown. Let cake cool. Frost with cream cheese frosting. Store cake in refrigerator.

Davey & Earline

CONDIMENTS
MISCELLANEOUS

Happy 79th Birthday ~ Ms. Earline

Randy & Donna Corley

Jamie & Allison Holder

Charles Holder

Cleo & Faye McCormick

We Love You!

PERFECT SEASONING

6 oz. garlic salt
6 oz. onion salt
6 oz. celery salt
1 tsp. red pepper
2 tsp. black pepper
2 tsp. paprika
1 tsp. chili powder

Mix well together. Store in tightly closed container.

RUN OUT OF BAR-B-Q SAUCE RECIPE

1 qt. catsup
1 cup corn syrup (light or dark)
¼ cup Worcestershire sauce
¼ cup sugar

Mix well. It is good on steak, chicken, ribs, and hamburger cooked on the grill.

CANNED PEACHES

10 lb. ripe peaches
2 cups water
3 lb. sugar

Peel peaches. Cut in half. Remove seed. Leave peaches in halves or cut. Rinse peaches to remove peach fuzz. In saucepan add peaches, sugar, water, and cook until tender. Place peaches and juice in sterilized jars. Seal tight.

PEPPER PECANS

3 T. butter
2 tsp. Worcestershire sauce
½ tsp. hot pepper sauce
2 cups pecan halves
dash of pepper (red)
salt

In a small pan, melt butter. Stir in Worcestershire sauce, pepper sauce and pepper. Add pecans. Spread in shallow baking pan. Bake in 300 degree oven for 20 minutes stirring occasionally. Afterwards, sprinkle with salt if desired.

PEPPER JELLY

⅓ cup jalapeno pepper
1 ⅓ cup bell pepper
6 ½ cups sugar
1 ¼ cups vinegar
6 oz. pkg. certo
3 drops green food coloring

Blend jalapeno pepper and bell pepper in food processor. Mix all ingredients together except for certo. Bring to boil one minute and reduce heat and cook for five minutes. Remove from heat and add certo. Stir and pour jelly in clean jars. This is very good on pork meat and dry peas and beans, to name a few.

FIG PRESERVES

1 gal. figs, trimmed and washed
2 lemons
1 box Sure-Jell
5 Lb. sugar

Place washed and trimmed figs in saucepan or large pot. Cover with sugar and let stand overnight or at least 8 hours. Figs will make its own juice. Place over high heat and bring to a rolling boil about 15 minutes. Slice lemons over figs. Remove lemon seeds. Pour in Sure-Jell and let cook until syrup is thick, stirring occasionally. Reduce heat for this will burn easily. Spoon figs into clean hot jars and seal. Use pint or ½ quart jars.

PEACH PRESERVES

May be canned the same way.

PEAR PRESERVES

Walter Phillips

May be canned the same way.

148

PICKLED PEACHES

10 lbs. firm ripe peaches, but not soft
5 lbs. sugar
1 qt. vinegar
1 tsp. whole cloves

Peel peaches. Combine sugar, vinegar, cloves and bring to a boil. Add peaches and let boil until they begin to get tender. Do not over cook. Peaches will fall off the seed. Place peaches in hot sterilized jars. Pour hot syrup over peaches and seal.

BREAD & BUTTER PICKLES

4 lb. cucumbers, sliced ¼ inch
3 onions, sliced
½ cup coarse salt
5 cups sugar
5 cups cider vinegar
1 ½ tsp. turmeric
1 ½ tsp. celery seeds

Cover cucumbers, onions and salt with cold water and ice cubes. Let stand about 3 hours. Do not use metal containers. Mix sugar, vinegar, turmeric and celery seeds and simmer 30 minutes. Pour cold water off cucumbers and pack in jars. Cover with hot liquid. Process 10 minutes in hot water bath.

Maudie Massey
Freeport, Illinois

Cedric Glenn & Russ Blakeney

COMPANY BEST PICKLES

10 medium cucumbers
8 cups sugar
2 T mixed spices
5 tsp. salt
3 cups cider vinegar

Cover whole cucumbers with boiling water. Allow to stand until next morning. Drain and slice into ½ inch pieces. Combine sugar, spices, salt, vinegar. Bring to boiling and pour over cucumbers. Let stand 2 days and on third day bring to boiling and seal in hot, sterilized jars. Makes 7 pints.

Geraldean Jones
Freeport, Illinois

PEAR PRESERVES #2

1 bushel basket fresh canning pears (there is a difference)
12 cups sugar
3 lemons
2 boxes Sure-Jell

Peel and slice pears away from the core. Wash pears and place in large canning pot. Pour sugar over top of pears. Let stand overnight at room temperature. Cook pears about 1 hour on top of stove. Add sure jell and sliced lemons. Let boil hard until juice is thick like syrup. Put in hot sterilized jars and seal.

George Barlow - The Noni Juice Man
Picture of Health

150

FAMILY REUNION PUNCH

6 ½ cup sugar
4 cups water
4 - 3 oz. boxes lemon gelatin
2 - 6 oz. cans frozen orange juice
2 - 6 oz. cans lemon juice
2 - 48 oz. cans pineapple juice
1 ½ oz. almond extract
4 qts. ginger ale or Sprite

Combine sugar and water in pot. Cook until sugar is dissolved and mixture is syrupy. Add gelatin. Stir until dissolved. Add fruit juices and 1 gallon water. Add almond extract. Put into container and freeze until thick and slushy. When ready to use, pour ½ mixture and ½ ginger ale or sprite in punch bowl and serve. Instead of freezing mixture, you can use ice or ice rings.

My son Melvin with
his sons Chris & Melvin 3rd

ICED TEA SPECIAL

1 gal. water
2 ½ cups sugar
about 20 tea bags

Bring water to boiling point, add tea bags and remove from heat. Cover and let steep 10 minutes. Remove tea bags and add sugar. Serve over ice cubes. May be served with lemon slices.

ICED TEA
(one gallon)

12 tea bags (I prefer Rainbow.)

Bring water to boiling point and remove from heat. Throw in tea bags and cover with lid. Let steep for 15 minutes and remove tea bags. Add 1 ½ cups sugar. Serve over ice cubes.

FOURTH OF JULY TEA

Bring 1 ½ quarts water to boiling point. Put in 8 tea bags. Steep about 5 minutes in large clean pot. Add tea, 2 ½ cups orange juice, ¼ cup lemon juice, 2 cups pineapple juice. Finish by adding 3 trays of ice cubes. Place in refrigerator. Will last several days.

Birds of a feather flock together

PARTY PUNCH

2 jars cherries and juice
3 cups sugar
3 lemons, sliced
3 oranges, sliced
1 lg. can pineapple juice
2 qts. water
2 pkg. strawberry jello

Mix all together. Serve over crushed ice.

LEMONADE - DAVEY'S STYLE

½ gallon cold water
3 cups sugar
3 scoops ice
½ cup lemon juice
1 pkg. lemon Kool-aid

Mix all together. Serve over ice cubes.

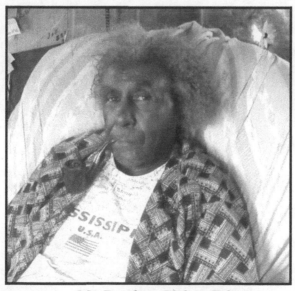

My Brother Clifton Edison

RECIPE INDEX

CAKES/COOKIES

CONDIMENTS/ MISCELLANEOUS

GUEST
LIST

DAVEY'S CUSTOMERS COME FROM ALL OVER THE WORLD!!!

Joe Griffin, Jr. . . . . Eveleth, Minnesota
Bobbie Mathis . . . . New York City, New York
John Mutchler . . . . Houston, Texas
David Griffith . . . . Houston, Texas
Clestine Davis . . . . Erie, Pennsylvania
Tom Harris . . . . Memphis, Tennessee
Scott Hicks . . . . Olive Branch, Mississippi
James E. Johnson . . . . Moulton, Alabama
Edna Oreno Davis . . . . Chicago, Illinois
Dale Bray . . . . Decatur, Illinois
Mr. & Mrs. Johnnie Newcomb . . . . Mesa, Arizona
Mary Ann LaRoche . . . . Pittsburgh, Pennsylvania
David O. Gibbon, Esq. . . . . Salt Lake City, Utah
Jennifer Gibbon Seal . . . . Meridian, Mississippi
Shelly Coats . . . . Louin, Mississippi
Zida Grayson . . . . Ellisville, Mississippi
Nita Johnson . . . . Jackson, Mississippi
Kathryn Smith . . . . Montrose, Mississippi
Laura Turner . . . . San Francisco, California
Joyce Turner . . . . Chico, California
Shirley Jennings . . . . Esparto, California
Lori Jennings . . . . Woodland, California
Frank & Rosie Vidalis . . . . Woodland, California
Thoj Stromsnes . . . . Andenes, Norway
Alexei L-de Castro . . . . Sao Paulo-Sp, Brazil
Linnea Newmon . . . . Chestertown, New York
Randy Sesars . . . . Turlock, California
Warren Shippen . . . . New Orleans, Louisiana
Walter Smallwood . . . . Mobile, Alabama
Sheila White . . . . Ellisville, Mississippi
P.J. Graham . . . . Stringer, Mississippi
Walter & Linda Smallwood . . . . Mobile, Alabama
Lakyn F. . . . . Laurel, Mississippi

DAVEY'S CUSTOMERS COME FROM ALL OVER THE WORLD!!!

David Jones . . . . Louin Mississippi
Lola L. . . . . .Laurel, Mississippi
Skeyes . . . . .Laurel, Mississippi
Karl & Bettye Seepe . . . . .Clinton, Mississippi
Juanita Trucano . . . . Goudan, Minnesota
Juan Jimenez Martinez . . . . .Santiago de Cuba, Cuba
Jeny Hutchinson . . . . Jackson, Mississippi
Louis Blaine Kihodeaux . . . . .Crowley, Louisiana
Linda Robinson . . . . Portola, California
Percy Sledge . . . . .Baton Rouge, Louisiana
Beverly Richardson . . . . Jackson, Mississippi
Brookes Eiler . . . . .Irving, Texas
Joe & Dodie LaCorte . . . . Jamul, California
Chuck Cooper . . . . Brandon, Mississippi
Dave Wilson . . . . .Mount Vernon, Washington
Myeez Ahmal . . . . .Mount Vernon, Washington
Thomas J. Perry . . . . Chicago, Illinois
Bryan Welch . . . . Memphis, Tennessee
David Brand . . . . .Biloxi, Mississippi
Kathi Jackson . . . . .Diamondhead, Mississippi
Thomas Cantwell . . . . .Omaha, Nebraska
Bob warren . . . . .Troy, New York
Tom Frenyea . . . . Troy, New York
Paul Prevost . . . .
Russ Tompkins . . . . .Schultzville, New York
Ron Branto . . . . .Saratoga, New York
Judy Denson . . . . Hattiesburg, Mississippi
Ernie Nivens . . . . .Gastonia, North Carolina
Rosemary Payne . . . . Charlotte, North Carolina
R.A. . . . . Atlanta, Georgia
Ron Meredith . . . . Atlanta, Georgia
Willie Keith . . . . Rochester, New York
Rev. Wayne Dubose . . . . Baton Rouge, Louisiana

DAVEY'S CUSTOMERS COME FROM ALL OVER THE WORLD!!!

Omer & Annette . . . . Newton, Mississippi

Timothy E. Spear . . . . Parker, Colorado

A. B. Farris, Jr. . . . . Ridgeland, Mississippi

Ruth Edmondson . . . . Volcano, California

Mark Berdwell . . . . Madison, Indiana

Jim F. . . . . Madison, Indiana

Dan Forgues . . . . Reno, Nevada

James Miles . . . . Hoamo, Louisiana

Truman Rousseau . . . . Biloxi, Mississippi

John Connolly . . . . Madison, Indiana

Carl Ambuster . . . . Cincinnati, Ohio

Eril C. . . . . Union, South Carolina

Billy Whiskers . . . . Lumberton, Mississippi

Trish Ankeny . . . . Honolulu, Hawaii

Davy Banning . . . . Shelbyville, Illinois

Carrard Haygood . . . . Detroit, Michigan

Laura Belle Moncrief . . . . Columbus, Ohio

Inez Moncrief . . . . Columbus, Ohio

Kent, Faye & Cliff Prince . . . . New Orleans, Louisiana

Greg Moore . . . . Tuscaloosa, Alabama

Shelby Cummins . . . . Neosho, Missouri

Catie Cummins . . . . Neosho, Missouri

Chip Pickering . . . . Washington, D. C

Keith & Amy Youngblood . . . . Bay Springs, Mississippi

Jack & Valelis Crosby . . . . Lake, Mississippi

Edward Nelson . . . . Newton, Mississipp

Joy McDonald . . . . Lena, Mississippi

Larry Trotter . . . . Madison, Mississippi

Mellessia Rose . . . . Glen Rose, Texas

Byron Stinson . . . . Glen Rose, Texas

Waynett Brown . . . . Lucedale, Mississippi

Rev. Bill Marble . . . . Bay Springs, Mississippi

Billy Richardson . . . . Brandon, Mississippi

DAVEY'S CUSTOMERS COME FROM ALL OVER THE WORLD!!!

Stoney Powell . . . . Falkville, Alabama
Chad Anderson. . . . . .Hattiesburg, Mississippi
Dusty Halbrooks. . . . . Falkville, Alabama
Billy Denson . . . . Decatur, Alabama
Larry Blakeney . . . . Laurel, Mississippi
Rich Eberhart . . . . .Laurel, Mississippi
Tandy Roberson . . . . .Laurel, Mississippi
Steve Taylor . . . . .Hattiesburg, Mississippi
Dr. Paul A Little . . . . Brandon, Mississippi
Dr. Samuel H. McLaurin, Jr. Bay Springs, Mississippi
Lee Upton . . . . .Stringer, Mississippi
Bobby Seymour . . . . .Gulfport, Mississippi
Wayne Waltman . . . . .Pass Christian, Mississippi
Gene Waltman . . . . .Pass Christian, Mississippi
Randy Johnson . . . . .Stringer, Mississippi
Charlie Goodman . . . . .Cuba, Alabama
Ember Pitts . . . . .Newton, Mississippi
Mark George . . . . .Newton, Mississippi
Marcia Taylor . . . . .Homewood, Mississippi
Melvin Mack . . . . Laurel, Mississippi
D. L. Giegen, Jr. . . . . .Laurel, Mississippi
Roger H. Hill . . . . Hattiesburg, Mississippi
Billy Lewis . . . . Hattiesburg, Mississippi
Stacey M. Myers . . . . .Bay Springs, Mississippi
Norma Jean Lowe . . . . Union, Mississippi
Charlie Carlisle . . . . .Water Valley, Mississippi
Elon Espey . . . . Hickory, Mississippi
Kevin Jordan . . . . Laurel, Mississippi
Danny Speadey . . . . .Soso, Mississippi
Johnny Johnson . . . . Laurel, Mississippi
Ahrles Miller . . . . .Laurel, Mississippi
John McClain . . . . Brandon, Mississippi
Keith Sims . . . . Bay Springs, Mississippi

DAVEY'S CUSTOMERS COME FROM ALL OVER THE WORLD!!!

Mr. & Mrs. George Coleman	Newton, Mississippi
Joe Allen	Bethesda, Ohio
Zach Allen	Baton Rouge, Louisiana
Henry & Sue McCrory	Clarksdale, Mississippi
Max James	Bay Springs, Mississippi
Gary Puckett	Charlotte, North Carolina
Richard Puckett, Sr.	Slidell, Louisiana
Dave B. Johnson	Jones County Junior College; Ellisville, Mississippi
Floyd R. B. Jane Jr.	Jones County Junior College; Ellisville, Mississippi
Mike Simpson	Columbia, South Carolina
Charlie Stacey Grantham	New Hampshire
James Folan	Nesbit, Mississippi
Chack & Lynda Barfield	Hattiesburg, Mississippi
Col. Tom Edwards & Marie	Jackson, Mississippi
Debbie Wiles	Frederick, Missouri
Cathy Harmm	Hattiesburg, Mississippi
Dan Bowerina	Hattiesburg, Mississippi
Elsie Peel	Hattiesburg, Mississippi
Doris McLellans	Hattiesburg, Mississippi
Colleen Cameron	Hattiesburg, Mississippi
Mary Jean Saulters	Heritage United Methodist Church; Hattiesburg, Mississippi
Carolyne Paylor	First United Methodist; Wiggins, Mississippi
Cub Nelson	Heritage United Methodist Church; Hattiesburg, Mississippi
Helois Lowery	Hattiesburg, Mississippi
Frances Calhoun	Wesley Manor
Rebecca Pace	Hattiesburg, Mississippi
Joe & Sharon Pickel	Marow, Los Angeles
Scott Barnes	Clovis, California
Wallace Hubbard	New Technologies; Bay Springs Tel guest
Danco Browster	Atlanta, Georgia

DAVEY'S CUSTOMERS COME FROM ALL OVER THE WORLD!!!

Glen Holman . . . . Winter Springs, Florida
Mark Eubanks . . . . Philadelphia, Mississippi
Jason Bane . . . . Louisville, Mississippi
Brad Sellers . . . . Canton, Mississippi
Laurence Morri . . . . Flora, Mississippi
D. Thatcher . . . . Madison, Mississippi
David H. Richardson . . . . Ridgeland, Mississippi
Bill Banks . . . . Madison, Mississippi
Brad Casto . . . . Elkview, West Virginia
Mike, JoAnn, Joy & Alison Miller . . . . Mandeville, Los Angeles
Anthony Thorman . . . . Jackson, Mississippi
Bob Olson . . . . Tuscoloosa, Alabama
Ray, Debbo, Emily & Claire Pugh . . . . Louin, Mississippi
Sharon Wyatt . . . . Brandon, Mississippi
Arnold D. Knott Sr. . . . . Huntsville, Alabama
Diane White . . . . Huntsville, Alabama
Virginia N. Watts . . . . Laurel, MississippI
Texana McFarland . . . . Laurel, Mississippi
Joan Garver . . . . Brandon, Mississippi
Theresa Garver . . . .
Amanda Fendley . . . . Tuscaloosa, Alabama
Surgent Turner . . . . Tuscaloosa, Alabama
Tammy Fendley . . . . Tuscaloosa, Alabama
Roy Lea . . . . Pitkin, Los Angeles
Richard McDonald . . . . New Orleans; Los Angeles
Wendell Darby . . . . New Orleans; Los Angeles
Ray & Betty Gordy . . . . Tulsa, Arkansas
Harley & Billie Craven . . . . Newton, Mississippi
Sue Thurston . . . . Farmersville, Los Angeles
Raland Burks . . . . Petal, Mississippi
Nicky Shelton . . . . Olive Branch, Mississippi
Harry Patton . . . . Nitta Yuma, Mississippi
Chris Nutter . . . . Madison, Mississippi
Matt Mitchell . . . . Madison, Mississippi

DAVEY'S CUSTOMERS COME FROM ALL
OVER THE WORLD!!!

Lucius Brodi . . . . .McComb, Mississippi

Jini Perry . . . . .Raleigh, North Carolina

Gary Boatnron . . . . Jackson, Mississippi

Rev. Mart Hanna . . . . Laurel, Mississippi

Donald Pounders . . . . .Laurel, Mississippi

Bitt Tew . . . . Stringer, Mississippi

Samuel J. Pince . . . . .Laurel, Mississippi

Peggy Roper . . . . New Sunnerfield, Texas

A.S. Hennis . . . . Petal, Mississippi

Hal Ethridge . . . . .Hickory, Mississippi

Glenn Hendry . . . . .Stringer, Mississippi

L.G. Soley . . . . .Laurel, Mississippi

Dwight & Lynn Mims . . . . .Burns, Oregon

Lena M. Pilgram . . . . .Bay Springs, Mississippi

Charles & Frances Foole . . . . Greenville, D.C.

Walter & Susan Parker . . . . Laurel, Mississippi

Todd & Renae Shows . . . . Soso, Mississippi

Larry & Loyce Fulton . . . . Philadelphia, Mississippi

Roy Hardy . . . . .Houston, Texas

Lecreta Lewis . . . . Houston, Texas

Juvwell Bacigalupi . . . . Biloxi, Mississippi

Belinda Mims . . . . .Phoenix, Arizona

Walter and Nadine Maxwell . . . . .Mendenhall, Mississippi

Steve Clarke . . . . .Coral Springs, Florida

Marbert Nicholas . . . . Tavares, Florida

Eric Clarke . . . . .Boca Raton, Florida

Sallie Gray . . . . Laurderdale, Mississippi

Faye G. Michel . . . . West Point, Mississippi

Jim Landers . . . . .Cross Lanes, West Virginia

Mary A. Norris . . . . Texas

Peggy Jones . . . . Caledonia, Mississippi

Linda Way . . . . Little Rock, Mississippi

Tammy Gentry . . . . Little Rock, Mississippi

DAVEY'S CUSTOMERS COME FROM ALL OVER THE WORLD!!!

Buck Stringer . . . . .Bay Springs, Mississippi
Nulani Stringer . . . . .Bay Springs, Mississippi
Ann Fraza . . . . .Jackson, Mississippi
Jim Cartt . . . . Madison, Mississippi
Bill Barry . . . . Brandon, Mississippi
Buddy Mitcham . . . . .Madison, Mississippi
James Edwards . . . . .Jackson, Mississippi
Gary & Melanie Gilmore . . . . .Decatur, Mississippi
Evalyn & Bruno Karkula . . . . Fort Myers, Florida
Holly Bounds . . . . .Atlanta, Georgia
赵庭祥 . . . . .Shanghai, China
Mike Phair . . . . .Puyallup, Washington
Bill Franz . . . . .Monlatt, INC
Lena Hunt . . . . .Leesville, Los Angeles
Harry & Margaret Jones . . . . .Stringer, Mississippi
J.D. & Bonnie Thompson . . . . .Lena, Mississippi
Robert Wit . . . . .Jackson, Mississippi
Gorh Cole . . . . .Laurel, Mississippi
Jim, Emily, Amy, Joe, Dunagin . . . . McAlester
Bob & Nancy Price . . . . .Munhall, Pennsylvania
Bonnie Hastings . . . . Denver, Colorado
Jerry W. Sumrall . . . . Beaumont, Texas
Thomas & Sue Williams . . . . .Petal, Mississippi
Margaret Evans . . . . .New Orleans, Los Angeles
Wayne & Cristie Herring . . . . Tylertown, Mississippi
Red H. . . . .
Tim Dunaway . . . . .Piris, Mississippi
William Tynn . . . . Clinton, Mississippi
MGrtis C. Webb . . . . .Jackson, Mississippi
Todd Carter . . . . Slidell, Mississippi
Mike Reid . . . . Orange Beach, Alabama
Scott Caldwell . . . . Hattiesburg, Mississippi
Jarpe & Carrell Courtney . . . . Scalbey, Mississippi
Ruth & Ray Johnson . . . . Sutter Creek, California

DAVEY'S CUSTOMERS COME FROM ALL OVER THE WORLD!!!

Janice Brachy . . . . .Louin, Mississippi
Pepper Crutoher . . . . Jackson, Mississippi
RN Lufe . . . . Forest, Mississippi
Mike & Janet Lewis . . . . .Sandersville, Mississippi
Richard & Sarah Moore . . . . .Olive Branch, Mississippi
Juanita Saterfiel . . . . .Lake, Mississippi
Greg & Janet Stephens . . . . Ft. Wayne, Indiana
John & Jasmine Bilello . . . . Marion, Mississippi;
Pensacola, Florida
Jim Pittmon . . . . .Collinsville, Mississippi
Jon Knight . . . . .Dekalb, Mississippi
Frank Blossman . . . . .Madison, Mississippi
Mark Kocber . . . . Peoria, Illinois
Steve Thorson . . . . Peoria, Illinois
John and Ginger Meador . . . . Hattiesburg, Mississippi
Bryon & Nita Buckley . . . . .Collins, Mississippi
Charlie Buckley . . . . Collins, Mississippi
David Weatherton . . . . Tyler, Texas
Randy Hauser . . . . .Nashville, Texas
Stan Runnsls . . . . .Laurel, Mississippi
Chasley Windham . . . . .Laurel, Mississippi
Robert Nicholas . . . . .Green Bay, Wisconsin
Sery Forny . . . . Meridian, Mississippi
Bufford Crain . . . . .Mevelin, Mississippi
George E & Betty Cawsey . . . . .Petal, Mississippi
Mike & Jon Roberts . . . . Ellisville, Mississippi
Joe Evelyn & Jack Johnson . . . . .Croluralia, Mississippi
Ray T. Haxouls . . . . .Mabonk, Texas
Hayden Braddock Tifton . . . . Georgia
Steve Bowles . . . . Tupelo, Mississippi
Doug Purvis . . . . Frisco City, Alabama
Gret Taylor . . . . .Vossburg, Mississippi
Richard Spooner . . . . New Orleans; Los Angeles
DeWayne Seyx . . . . Jackson, Mississippi
Dale H Penson . . . . Edid, Oklahoma

DAVEY'S CUSTOMERS COME FROM ALL
OVER THE WORLD!!!

Byron & Sherry Gwen . . . . Jackson, Mississippi
Keith & Dease Green . . . . .Byran, Mississippi
George & Louise Land . . . . Sardis, Mississippi
Martha, Amy, John Goodwin . . . . .Senatobia, Mississippi
Laura Nash . . . . .Bow, Washington
Aaron Dearinger . . . . .Fishers, Indiana
Basem K. Toma . . . . .Raleigh, North Carolina
Brad Cocke . . . . Birmingham, Alabama
Harry A Locke . . . . .Man, Mississippi
Rick Bennett . . . . Bay Springs, Mississippi
Lillie Belle Dixon Campbell . . . . .Las Vagas, Nevada
Mr. Claude Marsh . . . . .Las Vagas, Nevada
Jim Mount . . . . Rittal Corp.;
                                                    Raleigh, North Carolina
Larry Ward . . . . .Stewart, Mississippi
Larry Wilkinson . . . . .Brookhaven, Mississippi
R.L. Denmark . . . . .Lucedale, Mississippi
Raymond R. Vaughn . . . . Aiken, South Carolina
T.L. Dunn . . . . .Jackson, Mississippi
Odessa Gant . . . . Aur., Alaska
William & Barbara French . . . . .Biloxi, Mississippi
Sarah Wallen . . . . Gulfport, Mississippi
Ginger Creel . . . . Biloxi, Mississippi
H.M. Harris, Jr. . . . . Carreie, Mississippi
Denise Smith . . . . .Petal, Mississippi
Dot Wilson . . . . .Taylorsville, Mississippi
Lee Potts . . . . Gulfport, Mississippi
Marcus Robinson . . . . .Hattiesburg, Mississippi
Bobby R. Meor . . . . Geraldine, Alabama
Billy Houser . . . . Crossville, Alabama
Keith Ashley . . . . Albertsville, Alabama
Robert Munn . . . . Newton, Mississippi
Christine Duncan . . . . .Crofton MD ;Washington DC
Dan Weaver . . . . .Kent Island, Maryland
Brecic Campbell . . . . Decatur, Mississippi

DAVEY'S CUSTOMERS COME FROM ALL OVER THE WORLD!!!

T. A. . . . . *New York City, New York*

Alex Andrusevich . . . .*New York City, New York*

John Renny . . . . *San Antonio, Texas*

Bobby Miler . . . .*Shreveport, Louisiana*

Terrell & Ann Tollison . . . . *Mount Olive, Mississippi*

Bill & Jill Miller . . . . *Mount Olive, Mississippi*

Robert Boyer . . . . *Biloxi, Mississippi*

Kent L. Peacock . . . .*Omaha, Nebraska*

Babbs Richardson . . . .*Brandon, Mississippi*

Randy Kitchen . . . . *Augusta, Georgia*

Ron Pugh . . . .*Oldenburg, Germany*

Tues Pugh, Gramsch . . . .*Oldenburg, Germany*

Ken & Marine Vaughn . . . . *Taylorsville, Mississippi*

Wendell & Marjie Vaughn . . . .*Sandpoint, Idaho*

Clifford Sims . . . . *Weaver, Alabama*

John & Mechelle Barber . . . . *Lubbock, Texas*

Larry Bell . . . .*West Des Moines, Iowa*

Nelson Folse, Jr. . . . . *Thibodeaux, Louisiana*

Marv Deer . . . . *Urbandale, Iowa*

Joe Dupri . . . . *Thibodeaux, Louisiana*

Mary P. Jackson . . . .*Atlanta, Georgia*

Mary Beth Jackson . . . .*Atlanta, Georgia*

Betty Powell . . . .*Soso, Mississippi*

Bishop Oliver J. Edison . . . .*Des Moines, Iowa*

Jim Murray . . . .*Madison, Mississippi*

Lyle Barnes . . . .*Cowden, Illinois*

Bill Kovacich . . . .*Champaign, Illinois*

Simon Drummond . . . . *Birmingham, Alabama*
Atlanta, Georgia
Chicago, Illinois

Margaret Beck . . . . *Florence, Texas*

Dwana Beck . . . .*Florence, Texas*

May Dale Forest . . . . *Liberty Hill, Texas*

Chuck Paterson . . . .*Nacogdoches, Texas*

DAVEY'S CUSTOMERS COME FROM ALL
OVER THE WORLD!!!

Gary Patterson . . . . .Jackson, Mississippi

Rev. & Mrs. Ronald Robinson .Forest, Mississippi

Michael Applebaum . . . . .New Orleans, Louisiana

Carolyn Cowart . . . . New Orleans, Louisiana

Joyce Hodges . . . . .Chico, California

Bob Lorgas . . . . Atlanta, Georgia

Clint Joy . . . . .Atlanta, Georgia

Emma McGee . . . . Jackson, Mississippi

Lee Otis Bester . . . . .Brockton, Massachusetts

Aldora Benton . . . . .Rockford, Illinois

L. N. Craft . . . . .Rockford, Illinois

Zenola R Davis . . . . Tampa, Florida

Robert L. Davis . . . . Tampa, Florida

Roosevelt Davis . . . . .Cleveland, Ohio

Gary Pearson . . . . .Riverside, California

Roy Rossman . . . . .Hemet, California

Joey Gonce . . . . Florence, Mississippi

Larry Walker . . . . Philadelphia, Mississippi

Pat & Duncan McCaskey . . . . .Moss Point, Mississippi

Connie & Billy Rayner . . . . Moss Point, Mississippi

Mike Dewitt . . . . Memphis, Tennessee

Amalia Infonte . . . . .Aliconte, Spain

Rafael dos Santa Selecado . . . . Horizonte, Brazil

Lynette Enoch . . . . .Bronx, New York

S. Lawrence Fields . . . . .Bronx, New York

Cornell Enoch . . . . .Bronx, New York

Bobby McGlaston . . . . .Milwaukee, Wisconsin

Jim Grubbs . . . . .Stevens Point, Wisconsin

Steve Gassen . . . . .Gwinner, North Dakota

Lisa M. Futler . . . . Colorado Springs, Colorado

Bob Adkisson . . . . Monument, Colorado

Wolfjemy Deimel . . . . .Rheine, Germany

Rusty Fowler . . . . Memphis, Tennessee

DAVEY'S CUSTOMERS COME FROM ALL OVER THE WORLD!!!

Cliff Addison . . . . West Memphis, Arizona
Jeanette Davis . . . . Mobile, Alabama
Bob Holligan . . . . Washington, D. C.
Tony Bunch . . . . Mountain Home, Arizona
Terry Trebilcock . . . . Upland, California
Carol Vidimha . . . . Dooney, California
Maxine Manning . . . . Saint Joseph, Illinois
Nancy Kleiss . . . . Pesotum, Illinois
Clay Carley . . . . San Diego, California
Sam Fielden . . . . San Diego, California
David Ongemach . . . . Waupaca, Wisconsin
Weifard Kitchino . . . . Dade City, Florida
J. R. Kitchino . . . . Dade City, Florida
Rev James Fendlason . . . . Picayune, Mississippi
Billy Lewis . . . . Hattiesburg, Mississippi
Roger H. Hill . . . . Hattiesburg, Mississippi
Sammie Clark . . . . Adin, California
Larry Parks . . . . Gulfport, Mississippi
Emmett Gosnell . . . . Bethany, Illinois
Bob & Cindy Brader . . . . Los Angeles, California
Alabama Darley . . . . Laurel, Mississippi
Sam Altithon . . . . Dallas Texas
Eugene Delport . . . . South Africa
Jody & Jill Wagner . . . . Stillwater, Oklahoma
Randy D. . . . . Forest, Mississippi
Billy B. . . . . Magee, Mississippi
Stanford Young . . . . Waynesboro, Mississippi
John H. Belrig . . . . Meridian, Mississippi
B. R. . . . . Jackson, Mississippi
Marvin Oates . . . . Bay Springs, Mississippi
Johnny & Sheila Chapman . . . . Reno, Nevada
Ed McGhee . . . . Hammond, Louisiana
M. L. McKay . . . . San Diego, California

DAVEY'S CUSTOMERS COME FROM ALL OVER THE WORLD!!!

Jerry Henderson . . . .*Laurel, Mississippi*

Glenda Barrett . . . .*Decatur, Mississippi*

Habert H. Jones . . . .*Arcadia, Louisiana*

Grace H. Davis . . . .*Arcadia, Louisiana*

Amber Heflin Ockerbloom . . . .*Charlotte, North Carolina*

Tom Faccaf . . . .*Plano, Texas*

Del Crum . . . .*Hattiesburg, Mississippi*

Jim Young Hood . . . .*Baton Rouge, Louisiana*

Pappa Soul The Maharajah of the Blues from 102 WJKX . . .*Laurel & Hattiesburg, Mississippi*

Laura Runnels . . . .*Laurel, Mississippi*

Jolene G. Page . . . .*Blue Ridge, Mississippi*

Carol Diestilmeier . . . .*Jackson, Mississippi*

Donny R. Liuidsey . . . .*Silas, Alabama*

Jeff Noel . . . .*Slidell, Louisiana*

Brent Hatters . . . .*Wiggins, Mississippi*

Christopher Watkins . . . .*Hattiesburg, Mississippi*

Glen Shows . . . .*Beaumont, Mississippi*

Randy, Donna, & Taylor, Corley . . . .*Bay Springs, Mississippi*

David Smith . . . .*Amite, Louisiana*

Valerie Ulmer . . . .*Soso, Mississippi*

Mark Bullock . . . .*Chattanooga, Tennnessee*

Rusty Russell . . . .*Union, Mississippi*

Mark McCluna . . . .*Spring City, Tennessee*

Joe Slay . . . .*Dallas, Texas*

Joey Cooley . . . .*Laurel, Mississippi*

Johnny Thompson . . . .*Meridian, Mississippi*

Joe Westmoreland . . . .*Atlanta, Georgia*

Rickey Chance . . . .*Ocean Springs, Mississippi*

Laura Chance . . . .*Ocean Springs, Mississippi*

Richard Limmer . . . .*Tampa, Florida*

Chris Welch . . . .*Laurel, Mississippi*

David Wheat . . . .*Laurel, Mississippi*

Dave & Beverly Kelly . . . .*Jackson, Mississippi*

Rob Sandle . . . .*Hattiesburg, Mississippi*

DAVEY'S CUSTOMERS COME FROM ALL OVER THE WORLD!!!

Josh Webb . . . . .Quitman, Mississippi

Will McMillan .Newton, Mississippi

Jay Kellum . . . . .Baton Rouge, Louisiana

Song Soc Lee Yocuy Ja . . . . .Seoul, Korea

Yoon Koung Lee . . . . .Seoul, Korea

Hyua Juu Hm . . . . .Seoul, Korea

Joon Soo, Lee . . . . .Seoul, Korea

성 용 현 . . . . .Seoul, Korea

Buddy Special . . . . .Picayune, Mississippi

Bryan White . . . . .Picayune, Mississippi

Kevin Isaacson . . . . .Menominee, Michigan

Bob Shilts . . . . .Menominee, Michigan

Teresa Key . . . . .Jackson, Mississippi

Theonella Gross . . . . .Jackson, Mississippi

Madelin Green . . . . .Morton, Mississippi

Teresa Key . . . . .Jackson, Mississippi

Sean Revels .Brandon, Mississippi

John R. Bake Jr. . . . . .Raleigh, North Carolina

Dewayne Robiso . . . . .Enterprise, Mississippi

Steve Hill .Ridgeland, Mississippi

Alejandeo lara . . . . .San Luis Potosi, Mexico

Jose'Ledzma . . . . .San Lois Potosi, Mexico

Ma. Eugenla Tapla Ramirez . . . . .San Lois Potosi, Mexico

Gabriel Monsivais Ganer . . . . .San Lois Potosi, Mexico

Herbert & Jean Nettleton . . . . .Seminary, Mississippi

Don Correll . . . . .Picayune, Mississippi

Thomas McCardee . . . . .New Augusta, Mississippi

Carolyn McCardee . . . . .New Augusta, Mississippi

Wanda Simpson . . . . .Hattiesburg, Mississippi

James Doleman . . . . .Sullivan, Illinois

Gary Harris . . . . .Fillmore, South Carolina

Burna Lee Dobbs . . . . .Moss Point, Mississippi

Nadine Lowery .Moss Point, Mississippi

Doris Womble . . . . .Moss Point, Mississippi

Mike Jenkins . . . . .Stapleton, Alabama

DAVEY'S CUSTOMERS COME FROM ALL OVER THE WORLD!!!

Jenny Quave	Vancleave, Mississippi
Gus Styea	Stapleton, Alabama
Frances McKenzie	Sturgis, Mississippi
Diala Zitterman	Monroe, Michigan
Paul Ortheb	Lambertville, Michigan
Daniel L. Stewart	Anderson, Indiana
Luciell (Strongs) Phillips	Champaign, Illinois
Lee Youngblood	Hickory, Mississippi
Angela Faggert Cook	Dothan, Alabama
Yvonne Murray	Jackson, Mississippi
Dr. Rodney Kat	Jacksonville, Florida
Travis Lewis	
Ray Waters	Kansas City, Mossouri
Andrew Trotter	Madison, Mississippi
Paul Malry	Greenfield, Tennessee
David Fay	Tallahassee, Florida
Paul Wurmser	Tallahassee, Florida
Dr. Thomas S. Rowland & Staff	Laurel, Mississippi
G.A. "Buddy" Warren	Kenneswick, Washington
Barry Lee	Buford, Georgia
Grace E. Johnston	Mobile, Alabama
Chris Bloomfield	Wyandotte, Michigan
Vince Caligiuri	Toledo, Ohio
Johnny Cook	Meridian, Mississippi
Jimmy Sullivan	Meridian, Mississippi
Virginia Stillner	Deland, Florida
Rod Stillur	Deland, Florida
Shelly S. Shama	Hattiesburg, Mississippi
Chary Thames	
Mark Steve Dorab	Hattiesburg, Mississippi
Jerry & Jo Ann Harris	Savannah, Georgia
Ondrian Hampton	Florence, Mississippi
Exo Peagler	Florence, Mississippi
Georgie Read	Louin, Mississippi
Doric Harris	Louin, Mississippi

DAVEY'S CUSTOMERS COME FROM ALL OVER THE WORLD!!!

Jane Pritchett . . . . .Louin, Mississippi

Ceil Read . . . . .Louin, Mississippi

Benjie Turnage . . . . .Magee, Mississippi

Johnny Garner . . . . .Magee, Mississippi

Shea Bourland . . . . .Louisville, Mississippi

David Walters . . . . .Jackson, Mississippi

Donald Fortenberry . . . . .Magee, Mississippi

Roy O. Billhop . . . . .Jackson, Mississippi

Richard Knox . . . . .Meridian, Mississippi

Debbie Southwell . . . . .McAllen, Texas

Brent Irons . . . . .Meridian, Mississippi

Michael Smith . . . . .Meridian, Mississippi

Grady Yeger . . . . .Meridian, Mississippi

Phil Trimble . . . . .Tullahoma, Tennessee

Fred & Barbara Read . . . . .Louin, Mississippi

Eddie & Jeanette Culpepper . . . . .Pasadena, Texas

Cleve Altman . . . . .Wiggins, Mississippi

Thad David Jr. . . . . .Wiggins, Mississippi

Bettie Buchanan .Heidelberg, Mississippi

Nancy Mariduena . . . . .Heidelberg, Mississippi

Gloria Williams . . . . .Colorado

Calvin Williams . . . . .Colorado

Tommy Munn . . . . .Washington D.C

Henry Fletcher . . . . .Quitman, Mississippi

Tray "Frog" Roberts . . . . .Eucutta, Mississippi

Joc C. Zeaci . . . . .Wausau, Wisconsin

Lucy & Boots Rives .Jackson, Mississippi

Sid Toney . . . . .Terry, Mississippi

Jason Borilus . . . . .Clinton, Mississippi

Matt Brown . . . . .Clinton, Mississippi

David Gibbs . . . . .Clinton

Phillips, Henrietta & Hillman . . . . .Bay Springs, Mississippi

Bill Maily . . . . .Raymond, Mississippi

D.R. Bozeman . . . . .Flora, Mississippi

Keith Swain . . . . .Madison, Mississippi

DAVEY'S CUSTOMERS COME FROM ALL OVER THE WORLD!!!

Pamela LeCoq . . . . .Morganza, Louisiana

Betty Ramagos . . . . .Laurel, Mississippi

Marty Knotts . . . . .Austin, Texas

Glen A. Wesley . . . . .Orange, Texas

Nelly Schg . . . . .Denver, Colorado

Kathryn Watkins . . . . .Hattiesburg, Mississippi

Larry Watkins .Hattiesburg, Mississippi

David Weatherful . . . . .Tyler, Texas

Richard Jones . . . . .Philadelphia, Mississippi

David & Susan Byrd . . . . .Biloxi, Mississippi

James Ables . . . . .Ennis, Texas

Sam Walter . . . . .Waldosta, Georgia

Susan & Bob Webb . . . . .Houston, Texas

Lamar, Cindy Sue & MacAllen Houser . . . . .Elkton, Maryland

Fritz Norbury . . . . .Carthage, Missouri

Archie Anderson . . . . .Philadelphia, Mississippi

Johnny & Bobbie Walton . . . . .Pascagoula, Mississippi

Lisa Morgan . . . . .Brentwood, Tennessee

Tatiana Nemlin .Abidjan, Cote DIvoire

Lona La'Nett Mitchell . . . . .Canal Winchester, Ohio

Quinett M. Myers . . . . .Heidelberg, Mississippi

Worth Barliaw . . . . .Peel City, Alabama

Angela Sartor .New Orleans, Louisiana

Bubby Maggio . . . . .New Orleans, Louisiana

Ted Forbes . . . . .Biloxi, Mississippi

Julie Levy . . . . .Biloxi, Mississippi

Gary McCeli . . . . .Gulfport, Mississippi

Tyler McCile . . . . .Gulfport, Mississippi

Jerry and Jacki Young . . . . .Harvey, North Dakota

Lexi Erickerson .Decatur, Mississippi

Sam Brooks . . . . .Laurel, Mississippi

Peggy Guso . . . . .Biloxi, Mississippi

Alan Pruclet & Family . . . . .Perrysburg, New York

James & Lillian Cole Weiss . . . . .Poughquay, New York

DAVEY'S CUSTOMERS COME FROM ALL OVER THE WORLD!!!

Donnie G. Cole . . . . .Bronx, New York

Maxey Peterson . . . . .Sturgis, Mississippi

Jerry Blackwell . . . . .Coto De Caza, California

Clyde & Nell Slade . . . . .Chunchula, Alabama

Ronnie H. Dobbs . . . . .Dunwoody, Georgia

Bettye Dobbs . . . . .Decatur, Mississippi

Buster Slay . . . . .Fitzpatrick, Alabama

Napolean Steele . . . . .Prattville, Alabama

Edward E. Clinton . . . . .Prattville, Alabama

Sidney & Mike Stevens . . . . .College Station, Texas

Diana Fenson . . . . .Hemer, California

David Gainey . . . . .Homewood, Mississippi

Brent Wade . . . . .Lorena, Mississippi

Tom & Billie Howell . . . . .Merigold, Mississippi

Dick & Harriet Myers . . . . .Collinsville, Tennessee

Victor V. Maridvena . . . . . . .Gunyaquil-Ecuador, South America

Richard Cook .Heidelberg, Mississippi

Mike Jenkins . . . . .Jackson, Mississippi

Lauri Jokela . . . . .Finland

Ruby Clare Harvey . . . . .Osyka, Mississippi

Erica Cheeks . . . . .Laurel, Mississippi

Donnell & Mary Chehane . . . . .D'Iberville, Mississippi

Pore Walloy . . . . .Brandon, Mississippi

Ayre Styler . . . . .Brandon, Mississippi

Rev. Henry Flowers . . . . .Jacksonvelle, Arkansas

Mike & Teresa Robertson . . . . .Ellisville, Mississippi

Betty McNab . . . . .Valparaise, Florida

Mary Ann Hailey . . . . .Meridian, Mississippi

Robin Miling . . . . .Decatur, Mississippi

William B. Kidd . . . . .Columbus, Mississippi

Sarah E. Evans .Taylorsville, Mississippi

Jerel Wade . . . . .Laurel, Mississippi

Sarah Catherine Evans . . . . .Taylorsville, Mississippi

Bradley Evans .Taylorsville, Mississippi

DAVEY'S CUSTOMERS COME FROM ALL OVER THE WORLD!!!

Lynn Evans . . . . *Taylorsville, Mississippi*

H. L. and Margie Bailey . . . . *Pensacola, Florida*

Gustavo Salazar . . . . *Laurel, Mississippi*

Betty Johnson . . . . *Raleigh, Mississippi*

Nancy Manduena . . . . *Ecuador, South America*

Mr. & Mrs Jefferson Duckworth . . . . *Los Angeles, California*

John Walters . . . . *Mulb, Florida*

Erickson Whaleg . . . . *Knoxville, Tennessee*

Randy & Cindy Reynolds . . . . *Forest, Mississippi*

R Kevin & Patty Reynolds . . . . *Forest, Mississippi*

Brad & Kim Peterson . . . . *Forest, Mississippi*

Wayne & Susan Lewis . . . . *Quitman, Mississippi*

Grace Lewis . . . . *Pachuta, Mississippi*

Debbie Smith . . . . *Laurel, Mississippi*

Glynn & Sandra Rea . . . . *Moss Point, Mississippi*

George & Jerrie Martin . . . . *Moss Point, Mississippi*

Lori Graham . . . . *Brandon, Mississippi*

Tracy Carter . . . . *Alabaster, Alabama*

Nancy Robertson . . . . *Sylvan Springs, Alabama*

Vressre Hines . . . . *Purvis, Mississippi*

Sylvia Rolison . . . . *Perkinston, Mississippi*

Kujo Kerterkami 注業管 . . . . *Tokyo, Japan*

Dr. and Mrs. John L Cash . . . . *Newton, Mississippi*

David & Sheila Gainey . . . . *Homewood, Mississippi*

Neal & virginia Goree . . . . *Homewood, Mississippi*

Jason & Adele Mahore . . . . *Petal, Mississippi*

Horace Deaton . . . . *Columbia, Mississippi*

Carl Wooley . . . . *Morton Mississippi*

Eunice Wooley . . . . *Morton, Mississippi*

Margie Simmons . . . . *Louin, Mississippi*

Bonnie Lewis . . . . *Forest, Mississippi*

Al & Barbara Deaton . . . . *Decatur, Mississippi*

E. Dee Quinnelly . . . . *Bay Springs, Mississippi*

Kris Sanchez . . . . *Maureps, Louisiana*

DAVEY'S CUSTOMERS COME FROM ALL OVER THE WORLD!!!

Steven Schumaker . . . .*Baton Rouge, Louisiana*

Dan Shoemaker . . . .*Peoria, Illinois*

Jay Rowley . . . .*Decatur, Illinois*

Cherie Schmidt . . . .*Aurora, Illinois*

Reginald Gavhan . . . .*Javtoon, Mississippi*

David Holloway . . . .*Clinton, Mississippi*

Charles Beard . . . .*Florence, Mississippi*

Jack Smith . . . .*Garner, North Carolina*

Willard & Ruby Harvey . . . .*Osyka, Mississippi*

Vivian Cheeks . . . .*Ellisville, Mississippi*

Vester Elzey . . . .*Soso, Mississippi*

Alice J. Bolton . . . .*Soso, Mississippi*

Virgil & LaKerne Elbey . . . .*Red Oak, Texas*

Tommy & Charles Shetel . . . .*Crossett, Arkansas*

Lafayette Ruffin . . . .*Fundoosa, Alabama*

Mark Bond . . . .*Bellville, Texas*

Chuck Thompson . . . .*Amite, Lousiana*

Don Taylor . . . .*Amite, Louisiana*

Odessa Dixon . . . .*Grand Bay, Alabama*

(Bubba) Olden Denbury . . . .*Pasadena, California*

Jerry Young . . . .*Wahsington, Illonois*

Paula Lindsey . . . .*Plano, Illinois*

Sharon Fendley . . . .*Friendswood, Texas*

Mickey T. Black . . . .*Greenwood, Mississippi*

Roger & Imadine Moore . . . .*Jackson, Mississippi*

Lula Pugh Hoskin . . . .*Newton, Mississippi*

Michael Hewitt . . . .*Ocala, Florida*

Annie Pearl Parvin . . . .*Gulfport, Mississippi*

John, Shelly, Nicole & Heather Daley . . . . . .*Vancleave, Mississippi*

Robert, Glenda & rindy Dawkins . . . .*Gautiet, Mississippi*

Stacy & Wade . . . .*Hattiesburg, Mississippi*

Greg M. Ford . . . .*Gulfport, Mississippi*

Larry Clay . . . .*Newton, Mississippi*

DAVEY'S CUSTOMERS COME FROM ALL OVER THE WORLD!!!

Tophea Cougdon . . . . .Fishers, Indiana

Ron Sentry . . . . .Cicero, Indiana

Jimmy Adams . . . . .Tuscaloosa, Alabama

Annette Boyd . . . . .Portersville, Mississippi

Robert H. Butler . . . . .Rochester, New York

Martin Butler . . . . .Clinton, Mississippi

Bea Bronch . . . . .Jackson, Mississippi

Beverly W. Hoga .Tougaloo, Mississippi

Gary Anderson . . . . .Jackson, Mississippi

Roy DeBury . . . . .Jackson, Mississippi

Jason S. Moore . . . . .Birmingham, Alabama

Steve Barnhardt . . . . .Harrisburg, North Carolina

Kaye Dyess . . . . .Bay Springs, Mississippi

Rick Beggerly . . . . .Jackson, Mississippi

Stacey Boykin . . . . .Forest, Mississippi

Pat McCraw . . . . .Laurel, Mississippi

Dione McAndrews . . . . .Heidelberg, Mississippi

Nora Bustin . . . . .Laurel, Mississippi

Mike Caroth . . . . .Valdosta, Georgia

John Bunton . . . . .Valdosta, Georgia

Robert Bryant . . . . .Valdosta, Georgia

Frank Garczynsia . . . . .Bay Springs, Mississippi

Darrell Holifield . . . . .Laurel, Mississippi

Richard Hernandez . . . . .Russellville, Mississippi

Gene Chamblin . . . . .Houston, Texas

Gilda Taylor . . . . .Arden, North Carolina

Darryl Michael . . . . .Fremont, California

Pat Michael . . . . .Freemont, California

Bob Michael . . . . .Freemont, California

Marilyn Kay Jackson . . . . .Riverside, California

Bill Pinson .Crystal Springs, Mississippi

John McClure . . . . .Newton, Mississippi

Jenny Huddleston . . . . .Canton, Mississippi

Jesse Thomas . . . . .Choctaw Tribal Council

DAVEY'S CUSTOMERS COME FROM ALL OVER THE WORLD!!!

Wayne & Barbara Heschnaier . . . . .Picayune, Mississippi

Ray Hodson . . . . .Portland, Oregon

Dean S. Richard . . . . .Portland, Oregon

Eile Brookes . . . . .Irving, Texas

Cynthia Jackles . . . . .Juno Beach, Florida

Sharon Woods . . . . .Tuscaloosa, Alabama

Mark Hickman . . . . .Tuscaloosa, Alabama

Ronnie Rigney . . . . .Mobile, Alabama

Randy Lowe . . . . .Cottonwood, Arizona

Laura Levering . . . . .Cottonwood, Arizona

David & Sandy Tadlock . . . . .Forest, Mississippi

Susan Hankins . . . . .Forest, Mississippi

Linda Haden . . . . .Westlake Village, California

Dr. & Mrs. Neil Clark . . . . .Destin, Florida

Dr. Paul A. Resemlin . . . . .Lawrence, Kansas

Dr. Steve Pirraut . . . . .Lawrence, Kansas

Eddie & Jean Pickens . . . . .Chicago, Illinois

Michael Davis . . . . .Saint Pete, Florida

Rick & Andrea Guddels . . . . .Saint Pete, Florida

Dr. & Mrs. Fred McDowell . . . . .Edinburg, Texas

Jim McFarline . . . . .Atlanta, Georgia

Bill Chase . . . . .Jacksonville, Florida

John Reed . . . . .Independence, Kentucky

Dannie Smith . . . . .Union, Kentucky

Todd Steimer .Vancouver, Washington

Johnny Sims . . . . .Forest, Mississippi

Ben Martin . . . . .Olathe, Kansas

David Finch . . . . .Jackson, Mississippi

R. J. . . . . .Berliner, Poland

Minnie Demerson . . . . .Fontana, California

Steven E. Curfiss . . . . .Cincinnati, Ohio

J. D. & Mary Brothers . . . . .Waldron, Arizona

Thomas C. . . . . .New York

DAVEY'S CUSTOMERS COME FROM ALL OVER THE WORLD!!!

Aaron Wambolt . . . . .Bay Springs, Mississippi

Donna McQuay . . . . .Waterloo, Canada

Lou Cappa .London, Ontario, Canada

Enid Caravaggio . . . . .Islington, Ontario, Canada

Darrel Osborn . . . . .Tulsa, Oklahoma

Deau Osborn . . . . .Tulsa, Oklahoma

Sam & Linda Harris . . . . .Kilbourne, Louisiana

Calvin Hardy-Cox . . . . .Lakewood, California

Sally English . . . . .Carson, California

Tina & Larry Hastings . . . . .Mobile, Alabama

James McAdams . . . . .Hattiesburg, Mississippi

Brenda Wallace .Beaumont, Mississippi

Clyde A. Campbell . . . . .Farrell, Pennsylvania

Gwyn Bell . . . . .Farrell, Pennsylvania

H. Sattel . . . . .Ludwigshafen, Germany

Albert Sattel . . . . .Ludwigshafen, Germany

Stanley, Shelia & Laci McNeil . . . . .Cleveland, Mississippi

Anthony Collins . . . . .Tampa, Florida

Bobby Wilburn . . . . .Tuscaloosa, Alabama

Victor V. . . . . .Montreal, Canada

Barry Bennett . . . . .Tuscaloosa, Alabama

Jack Harris . . . . .Tampa, Florida

J. Bark . . . . .Hazlehurst, Mississippi

Bert Bagley . . . . .Hazlehurst, Mississippi

Percy Jordan . . . . .Canton, Mississippi

Tamia Hajny . . . . .Glen Rose, Texas

Shawn Hajny . . . . .Glen Rose, Texas

Dr. Billy Shows . . . . .Newton, Mississippi

Dorothy Palmer . . . . .Dalton, Illinois

Verstell Palmer, Jr. . . . . .Brandon, Mississippi

Gary & Mary Ann Puckett . . . . .Charlotte, North Carolina

Elois Taylor . . . . .Somerset, New Jersey

Latasha Sanders . . . . .Somerset, New Jersey

Ellis Chance . . . . .Saint Louis, Missouri

DAVEY'S CUSTOMERS COME FROM ALL OVER THE WORLD!!!

Eddie Luter . . . .*Laurel, Mississippi*

Anita Rahaim . . . .*Laurel, Mississippi*

Ralph Bryant . . . .*Bay Springs, Mississippi*

Carlos Labadia . . . .*Kitchener, Canada*

Brandi Labadia . . . .*Athens, Texas*

Jackie Brownlee . . . .*Laurel, Mississippi*

Mae Jones . . . .*Decatur, Mississippi*

Buddy Hester . . . .*Lornea, Mississippi*

Jackie Burkholder . . . .*McAllen, Texas*

John & Ann Cook . . . .*Meridian, Mississippi*

Gord Kelloway . . . .*Ontario, Canada*

Jason Rains . . . .*Dayton, Indiana*

Morris Ehrhant . . . .*Seneca, Missouri*

Bernardo Ayaca Jr. . . . .*Garland, Utah*

Leighton & Evelyn Reynolds . . . .*Laurel, Mississippi*

Clariece Kelly . . . .*Ovett, Mississippi*

Bill & Donnitta Williamson . . . .*Maple Valley, Washington*

Forrest & Jan Harter . . . .*Redway, California*

Michael S. Price . . . .*Laurel, Mississippi*

Rudolph Ellie . . . .*Flint, Michigan*

Quintiu Bauswell . . . .*Flint, Michigan*

Magee Jewel Ellis Hardy . . . .

John Crumpton Hardy Jr. . . . .

Gene Holbrook . . . .*Jackson, Mississippi*

Windsel & Carolyn Phillips . . . .

Patti & J.W. Holder . . . .*Louin, Mississippi*

Billy Huffmann . . . .*Jackson, Mississippi*

Audrey Webb . . . .*Moss Point, Mississippi*

Susan Ruschmeyer . . . .*Springfield, Oregon*

Richard & Edith Avenmarg . . . .*Bay Springs, Mississippi*

Sonny Nettles . . . .*Louin, Mississippi*

Wilmer & Ann Eby . . . .*Shippensburg, Pennsylvania*

Larry, Annette, Connor & Tayor Strite . . . .*Bay Springs, Mississippi*

Precilla Evans . . . .*Louin, Mississippi*

DAVEY'S CUSTOMERS COME FROM ALL OVER THE WORLD!!!

Eric Butler . . . . .Collinsville, Mississippi

Fonda Wilson Cliore . . . . .Eldorado, Illinois

Peggy Gaines . . . . .Newton, Mississippi

Littie Thiac . . . . .Bay Springs, Mississippi

Chalmos Herrin . . . . .Laurel, Mississippi

James & Annie Mary Price . . . . .Meridian, Mississippi

Rob & Debbie Laird . . . . .Lake, Mississippi

Oren Kaspi . . . . .Israel

Jeannie Rustin . . . . .Laurel, Mississippi

Jacques Chirac . . . . .Paris, France

Bill Knight . . . . .Dallas, Texas

Andy Hegwood . . . . .Dallas, Texas

Mike & Becky Fertitta . . . . .Dallas, Texas

Dr. Clyde L. Odom .Pachuta, Mississippi

Dot Lorne . . . . .Birmingham, Alabama

Sophia Rodrigues . . . . .Frisco, Texas

Richard & Gina Headrick . . . . .Laurel, Mississippi

Michael & Becky Ray . . . . .Keller, Texas

Jesus Galindo . . . . .Monterrey, Mexico

Lance Zichelberger . . . . .Forest, Mississippi

Rita Price . . . . .Pascagoula, Mississippi

Celeste Graham .Bay Springs, Mississippi

Sylvia Barlow . . . . .Moss, Mississippi

Justin Liu . . . . .Los Angeles, California

Ken Thornton (Incredible!) . . . . .Advanc, North Carolina

Matt Stringer . . . . .Memphis, Tennessee

Jimmy Whitfield . . . . .Kenner, California

Paul Glasgon . . . . .Metairie, Louisiana

Steve Sommer . . . . .Analeiu, California

Kay Bunnalu (Great Food!) . . . . .Meridian, Mississippi

Joleen Moore (Can't Beat It!) . . . . .Meridian, Mississippi

Vickey Cobb (Great!) . . . . .Lauderdale, Mississippi

Cathy Rush Slaton (Excellent!) . . . . .Meridian, Mississippi

DAVEY'S CUSTOMERS COME FROM ALL
OVER THE WORLD!!!

Peeler G. Lacey .... *Laurel, Mississippi*

Holley W. Lacey .... *Laurel, Mississippi*

Stephen Morrisin .... *Chattonnga, Tennessee*

Tommie Speights .... *Prentise, Mississippi*

Oscar & Elizabeth Welch .... *Laurel, Mississippi*

Mary Curry .... *Biloxi, Mississippi*

Bill Lewis .... *Newton, Mississippi*

Tex McFarland .... *Laurel, Mississippi*

Virginia N. Watts .... *Laurel, Mississippi*

Pat Throop .... *Laurel, Mississippi*

Marquerite Walker .... *Laurel, Mississippi*

Sarah Holyfield .... *Laurel, Mississisppi*

Perry Smith .... *Brookhaven, Mississippi*

Brain Aehnlich .... *Laurel, Mississippi*

John Lowe .... *Laurel, Mississippi*

Matt Shepherd .... *Hattiesburg, Mississippi*

Paul Wohlheter .... *Hattiesburg, Mississippi*

Mitch Sims .... *Jasper Co., Mississippi*

Brandon Swanson .... *Chicago, Illinois*

Micheal Terry .... *San Antonio, Texas*

Jerome King .... *Wazahachie, Texas*

Roberto Ortiz .... *Oklahoma City, Oklahoma*

Darryl Coleman .... *Florida, USA*

Lon McLaurin .... *Brandon, Mississippi*

Bobby Breakfield .... *Ellisville, Mississippi*

Brenda Barber .... *Ellisville, Mississippi*

Stan Neese .... *Madison, Mississippi*

Rev. J. & Dora Gardner .... *Mt. Olive, Mississippi*

Doug & Bethany Gatewood .... *Fort Lauderdale, Florida*

Jim & Linda Bahr .... *Dixon, Missouri*

David Huff .... *Forest, Mississippi*

Rev. Llyord Bustard .... *Charlotte, North Carolina*

Hayward Reed .... *Laurel, Mississippi*

Fay Reed .... *Laurel, Mississippi*

Rev. Terry Ladell Priester .... *Columbus, Mississippi*

Terry Ladell Priester, Jr .... *Columbus, Mississippi*

Torrence Joseph Priester .... *Columbus, Mississippi*

DAVEY'S CUSTOMERS COME FROM ALL OVER THE WORLD!!!

Randy McGilberry .... Mobile, Alabama
Dan & Jan Davis .... Leawood, Kanasas
Micheal Hunter .... Tampa, Florida
Robbie Edgar .... Ridgeland, Mississippi
Rebecca Gradert .... Geaesee, Illinois
Jessis & Dolores Odom .... Richton, Mississippi
Mary T. Gray .... Brandon, Mississippi
Michael McDonald, Jr. .... Florence, Mississippi
Davis Moore .... Sumrall, Mississippi
Davis Velcek .... Stewart, Mississippi
Ronnie Montague .... French Camp, Mississippi
Joyce Bond .... Meridian, Mississisppi
James M. Bond .... Meridian, Mississippi
Dawn Crenshaw .... Meridian, Mississippi
Marlene McMahan .... Daleville, Mississippi
Lee Moore .... Meridian, Mississippi
Joe. E. Moore .... Meridan, Mississippi
Lena Linton .... Meridian, Mississippi
Joel & Amy Slayter .... Moss Point, Mississippi
Pat Caldwell .... Laurel, Mississippi
Maydale Enloe .... Gladewater, Texas
Nancy Hall .... Monroe, Louisanna
Tom Buctilos .... Columbus, Mississippi
Aimee Cockerham .... Hamilton, Mississippi
Mark Vialers .... Columbus, Mississippi
Harold Hunter .... Tremonton, Utah
Don Carlopow .... Brighirm, Utah
Bob Finamore .... Orlando, Florida
Sabrina Ferrin .... Bountiful, Utah
Bro. Derrick Simmons .... Meridain, Mississippi
Rev. Leon & Paula Stewart .... Morton, Mississippi
Dan & Paula Stangle .... Vincennes, Indiana
Ken & Gwen Snider .... Decker, Indiana
Pat & Ken Cheek .... Kenai, Alaska
Shelby & Rene Sumerall .... Morton, Mississippi
Frankie Thornton .... Raleigh, Mississippi
Kathy Keith .... Moselle, Mississippi
Wayne Edward .... Meridian, Mississippi
Micheal "Gator Man" Ray .... Laurel, Mississippi

DAVEY'S CUSTOMERS COME FROM ALL OVER THE WORLD!!!

Captain Eagle ....
Dr. D ....
Currie ....
Rev. Orie J. Hudson, Sr. ....
Sister Mary Hudson ....
Orie J. Hudson, Jr. ....
Don Patterson ....Pachuta, Mississippi
Glenn Dunbar ....Brookhaven, Mississippi
Wade Thompson ....Jackson, Mississippi
Anne Mara Decker ....Jackson, Mississippi
Mr. & Mrs. Rupert Malone ....Picayune, Mississippi
Bernice Lurkens ....Hattiesburg, Mississippi
Lara Wells ....Waynesboro, Mississippi
David Wells ....Waynesboro, Mississippi
Trisha Keyes ....Laurel, Mississippi
Dale Keyes ....Laurel, Mississippi
Kelsey Keyes ....Clinton, Mississippi
Josh Dennis ....Ridgeland, Mississippi
Jamie & Nicole Smith ....Laurel, Mississippi
Hope Smith ....Laurel, Mississippi
Stewart Maxy ....Tupelo, Mississippi
Johnny Robbins ....Macon, Mississippi
Scott "Butterbean" Cash ....Macon, Mississippi
Annie Lou Robinson ....Newton, Mississippi
Dorothy Nicholson ....Memphis, Tennessee
Micheal Kossey ....Los Angeles, California
Myra Robinson ....Brandon, Mississippi
Curtis Robinson ....Brandon, Mississippi
Warren Robinson ....Newton, Mississippi
Anna Robinson ....Newton, Mississippi
Mitzi Stubbs ....Madison, Mississippi
Elise Robinson ....Lawrence, Mississippi
Wade & Nancy Robinson ....Ridgeland, Mississippi
Tommy Robinson ....Brandon, Mississippi
Micheal Herring ....Laurel, Mississippi
Windsel & Carolyn Phillips. ....
Patti & J.W. Holder ....Louin Mississippi

DAVEY'S CUSTOMERS COME FROM ALL
OVER THE WORLD!!!

Nancy & Larry Taylor . . . . *Laurel, Mississippi*

Patsy Walters . . . . *Ridgeland, Mississippi*

Bob Walters . . . . *Madison, Mississippi*

Sandi Walters . . . . *Mobile, Alabama*

Micheal Townsend . . . . *Cleo, Texas*

Cheryl Rainer . . . . *Laurel, Mississippi*

Ashley Dudley . . . . *Laurel, Mississippi*

Lavon Evans . . . . *Laurel, Mississippi*

Ron Taylor . . . . *Laurel, Mississippi*

David Sistenad . . . . *Laurel, Mississippi*

Robbie Watson . . . . *Oxford, Mississippi*

Phynester Hillie . . . . *Newton, Mississippi*

Annie Brooks . . . . *Quitman, Mississippi*

James C. Ct. Sr. . . . . *Meridian, Mississippi*

Dan Robertson . . . . *Newton, Mississippi*

Dot Kervin . . . . *Reform, Alabama*

Paula Robetson . . . . *Newton, Mississippi*

Milal A. Robertson . . . . *Newton, Mississippi*

Susie Campbell . . . . *Laurel, Mississippi*

Doris & Charles Hanchey . . . . *Laurel, Mississippi*

David & Laura Valentine . . . . *Pickens, Mississippi*

Kelton Valentioe . . . . *Newton, Mississippi*

Bobbye Rae Watters . . . . *Laurel, Mississippi*

Tommy Ray Watters . . . . *New York, New York*

Scott Wattt . . . . *Laurel, Mississippi*

Donald Hill . . . .

Ruth E. Lenoir . . . .

Tommy & Annie Wall . . . .

Maru Gibbs . . . .

Frank & Rosann Palerzzi . . . .

Bev Clark . . . .

Way & Linda Brown . . . .

Providence Maybarry . . . .

Judy Boutwel . . . .

Martin & Audery Stampers . . . . *Louin, Mississippi*

Ysidro & Carolyn Salviar . . . . *Hattiesburg, Mississippi*

Caron Byrd . . . . *Ridgeland, Mississippi*

DAVEY'S CUSTOMERS COME FROM ALL OVER THE WORLD!!!

Mike Morgan . . . . Laurel, Mississippi
Greg & Henry Fletcher . . . . Quitman, Mississippi
Wendel & Marilyn Stewart . . . . Ellisville, Mississippi
Joe & Doris Pates . . . . Sandersville, Mississippi
Jerry Baucum . . . . Forest, Mississippi
Diane Devine . . . . Forest, Mississippi
Rachel Span . . . . Jackson, Mississippi
C J Duckworth & Family . . . .
Elder & Sis. R.A. Hancock . . . . Winnsboro, Louisiana
Eddie Horn . . . .
Mike Vaughn . . . .
Daniel Lonsen . . . .
Frank & Jeaneth Shereck . . . . Bagley, Minnesota
Charles & Dorothy Uhland . . . . Lancaster, Pennsylvania
T. J. Chung . . . . Korea
Robert Pigeon . . . . Montreal, Canada
Richard Torres . . . . Redlands, California
Mick Grogan . . . . Dubin, Ireland
Jerry & Jean A Moore . . . . Tyler, Texas
Gerry Cringle . . . . Minneapolis, Minnesota
Tony & Laura Zupanie . . . . Strongsville, Ohio
R.P. & Magdlena Smith . . . . Bean Station, Tenneessee
Clifford & Margaret Thomas . . . . Louisville, Mississippi
Curt Harris . . . . Anderson, Indiana
Steve Massey . . . . Jackson, Mississippi
Jimmy L Ware . . . . Madison, Mississippi
James M Peoples . . . . Madden, Mississippi
Asa A Putnam . . . . Froest, Mississippi
Ben Noveck . . . . New Orleans, Louisiana
Dan Dodson . . . . Alexandria, Louisiana
Jeanetto & Joe Tramuta . . . . Biloxi, Mississippi
Jesse Pritchett . . . . West Memphis, Arkansas
Elbert Miller . . . . Kingsland, Arkansas
Ricky Crouse . . . . Kingsland, Arkansas
Steven Y Thou . . . . Singapore, China
Mike Underwood . . . . Orrville, Ohio
Butch Comer . . . . Niceville, Florida
Tracy Willis . . . . Bettendorf, Indiana
Jery Simmons . . . . Jackson, Mississippi

DAVEY'S CUSTOMERS COME FROM ALL OVER THE WORLD!!!

Tim & Doyllier Woolford . . . . Mabelvale, Arkansas
Anri Lacabellec . . . . Laurel, Mississippi
Mary Gregory . . . . Laurel, Mississippi
Eva CHeeks . . . . Soso, Mississippi
Brandi Fail Callison . . . . Denver, Colorado
Leanne Bartholet . . . . Akron, Ohio
Julia Kea . . . . Meridian, Mississippi
Bea McKowan . . . . Petal, Mississippi
Bob McKowan . . . . Petal, Mississippi
Gil Read . . . . The Woodlands, Texas
Virginia & Dale Read . . . . Flowood, Mississippi
Richard & Nilda Witty . . . . Laurel, Mississippi
Ralph T. Pinnior . . . . Loond, New York
Lora Gipson . . . . Brandon, Mississippi
Stephanie L Vest . . . . Pearl, Mississippi
Amy Smith . . . . Brandon, Mississippi
Pamela Huddleston . . . . Laurel, Mississippi
Dorthy Huddleston . . . . Soso, Mississippi
Carmen Perry Beaubeaux . . . . San Diego, California
Kathy Guznan . . . . Houston, Texas
Larry Hancock . . . . Jonesboro, Arkansas
Jerry Cox . . . . Jonesboro, Arkansas
Paul Lion . . . . Pass Christian, Mississippi
Justin Martin . . . . Brandon, Mississippi
Nicky Shelton . . . . Olive Branch, Mississippi
Ron Bailey . . . . Kosciusko, Mississippi
Ryan Kuklinski . . . . Eagam. Minnesota
Lucius Brook . . . . Jackson, Mississippi
Teresa Ross . . . . Jackson, Mississippi
ArlandPhillips . . . . Brandon, Mississippi
Tom Butler . . . . Clarksdale, Mississippi
Tim & Fay Martin . . . . Meridian, Mississippi
Jim & Patricia Brumfield . . . . Magnolia, Mississippi
Chistine Alexander . . . . Jayess, Mississippi
John Essex . . . . Independence, Missouri
Gus Sandoval . . . . Tuba City, Arizona
Art Yancey . . . . Birmingham, Alabama
Bayless Ydil . . . . Birmingham, Alabama
Randy Harrison . . . . Pulaski, Mississippi

DAVEY'S CUSTOMERS COME FROM ALL OVER THE WORLD!!!

Teresa Harrison . . . . .Pulaski, Mississippi
Thosmas Harrison . . . . .Pulaski, Mississippi
Allison Arender . . . .
Jimmy, Brenda, Clayton, & Alisha Arender . . . .
Charlie Harrison . . . .
Andrea Arender . . . .
Dick Cobb . . . . .Milwaukee, Wisconsin
Charlie Stacey . . . . .New Hampshire, USA
Mike Simpson . . . . Columbia, South Carolina
Stefeno Vhshouro . . . . .Hvar, Croatia
James Carty . . . . .Hattiesburg, Mississippi
J Wade, II . . . . .New Orleans, Louisiana
S. Yorden . . . . .Ayrshine, Scotland
Anne Penman . . . . .Ayrshine, Scotland
Ron Penman . . . . .Ayrshine, Scotland
Tammy Holcomb . . . . Waynesboro, Mississippi
Pete & Lenora Cochran . . . . Waynesboro, Mississippi
Jimmy Johnson . . . . Purvis, Mississippi
Guy West . . . . .Dallas, Texas
Larry Brashier . . . . .Austin, Texas
Tyna Smith . . . . Laurel, Mississippi
Gene & Barbara Kinard . . . . Marion, Mississippi
Brian K. Humble . . . . .Girard, Kansas
Joseph A. Faddul . . . .
Sylvia M. Jaddul . . . .
Jeff Miller . . . . .Jackson, Mississippi
Martha Simmons . . . . Brandon, Mississippi
Tommy Robinson .Brandon, Mississippi
Annie Lou Robinson . . . . .Newton, Mississippi
Warren & Ann Robinson . . . . Newton, Mississippi
Julius Harterough .Budapest, Hungary
Beth Scorbrough .Meridian, Missisppi
June Laing . . . . Clinton, Mississippi
David A, Bounds . . . . .Hattiesburg, Mississippi
James & Kathy Watts . . . . Brandon, Mississippi
John & Nora Doss . . . . Fort Walton Beach, Florida
Tony Ames . . . . .Tacoma, Washington
Bailey, Rosalind, & Ben Dixon . . . . Corvauis, Montana
Doug Miller . . . . .Tucson, Arizonia

DAVEY'S CUSTOMERS COME FROM ALL OVER THE WORLD!!!

Micah Hendry . . . . Ovett, Mississippi
Hong Kong Sik Kim . . . . Seoul, Korea
Seing Mth Park . . . . Seoul, Korea
Cat Ellis . . . . Brandon, Mississippi
Danny Jones . . . . Corinth, Mississippi
Randy Plowen . . . . .Shubuta, Mississippi
Bill & Debra Carter .Union, Mississippi
Toby & Sue Stringer . . . . Alvin, Texas
Bettye Stringer . . . . Alvin, Texas
Audrey Walley . . . . .Alvin, Texas
Shot & Cela Harbour . . . . Meridian, Mississippi
Will & Tracy Shannon . . . . .Muncie, Tenneessee
Jim & Dalene Hoff .Greenfield, Indiana
Phil & Andrea Benson . . . . .Muncie, Indiana
Rick & Darlene Mayatt . . . . .Daleville, Indiana
John & Luanna Robinson . . . . .Anderson, Indiana
Mike & Kathie Fox . . . . .Muncie, Indiana
Mary & Patsey Carpenter . . . . .Chunky, Mississippi
Larry Davis . . . . Houston, Texas
Matthew Warren . . . . Union, Mississippi
Carl & Henrietta Cravens . . . . Mtn. Home, Arkansas
Lonnie & Kate Warren . . . . Union, Mississippi
Tim & Dayller Wolford . . . . .Mabelvale, Arkansas
Jay Jolly . . . . Russell, Mississippi
Gloria West . . . . Seattle, Washington
Tony Rivers . . . . .San Diego, California
Vivian McNickles . . . . Waynesboro, Mississippi
Angela Sarris . . . . Atlanta, Georgia
Thomas Sarris . . . . Atlanta, Georgia
Paula Smith . . . . Stringer, Mississippi
Cindy Sanford . . . . Seminary, Mississippi
Rhonda Smith . . . . .Laurel, Mississippi
Brian Mitchell . . . . Hattiesburg, Mississippi
Cherly McQueen . . . . .Collins, Mississippi
Jennifer Musgrove . . . . Ellisville, Mississippi
Richard Johnston . . . . Hamilton, Mississippi
Chuck A. Norman . . . . .Meridian/Newton, Mississippi
Gina Thomas . . . . Conneaut Lake, Pennsylvania
Jerry Jones . . . . Soso, Mississippi

DAVEY'S CUSTOMERS COME FROM ALL OVER THE WORLD!!!

Brian Bunnell . . . . Richton, Mississippi
H. L. Fitley . . . . Laurel, Mississippi
Carol Minica . . . . Slidell, Louisiana
Lisa Claire Lewis Cantwell . . . . Sabillasville, Maryland
Nora & Tommy Jones . . . . Bay Springs, Mississippi
Bernard & Janet Gautier . . . . Pascagoula, Mississippi
Liz Davies . . . . Salt Lake Cith, Utah
Stephanie Maharrey . . . . Salt Lake City, Utah
Edd Johnson . . . . Birmingham, Alabama
C. Reynolds . . . . Waynesboro, Mississippi
Jeff Cluff . . . . Salt Lake City, Utah
Brandon Cluff . . . . Salt Lake City, Utah
Corey Cluff . . . . Salt Lake City, Utah
John Bell . . . . Laurel, Mississippi
Richard Witty, Jr. . . . . Gainesville, Florida
Ronnie & Angie Miley . . . . Homewood, Mississippi
Lacey Gainey . . . . Homewood, Mississippi
Joe Bergil . . . . Forest, Mississippi
Angela f. Rodriquez . . . . Frisco, Texas
Freddy Rodriquez . . . . Frisco, Texas
Sophia Rodriquez . . . . Frisco, Texas
Ronnie & Beth Bayliss . . . . Hattiesburg, Mississippi
Dallas Evans . . . . Laurel, Mississippi
Maisie Evans . . . . Laurel, Mississippi
Bridgette Anderson . . . . Taylorsville, Mississippi
Chris Hinton . . . . Calhoun, Mississippi
Richard Buckhautts . . . . Ellisville, Mississippi
Jamie & Randy Martin . . . . Lake, Mississippi
Haskel & Ella Graham . . . . Ellisville, Mississippi
Ricky Walker & Family . . . . Decatur, Mississippi
Kenneth, Cindy, Will,
   Russ & Samm Thompson . . . . Decatur, Mississippi
Don Boney . . . . Laurel, Mississippi
Noel A Rogan . . . . Laurel, Mississippi
ISG Ricky G. Brown . . . . Bay Springs, Mississippi
SPC Antonio McCullum . . . . Bay Springs, Mississippi
SGT Greg Shelby . . . . Bay Springs, Mississippi
SGT Arther Lee Barnett . . . . Bay Springs, Mississippi
Ron Fulcher . . . . Canton, Mississippi

DAVEY'S CUSTOMERS COME FROM ALL OVER THE WORLD!!!

Wayne Henson . . . . .Meridian, Mississippi
Michael Ingram . . . . Jackson, Mississippi
Kevin Hedgpeth . . . . Collinsville, Mississippi
Tim Mood . . . . .Madison, Mississippi
David Miranda . . . . Koster City, California
Natalie Copeland . . . . Goldsboro, Nevada
Harold & Marilyn Jackson & Delaney . . . . Riverside, California
David W. Ashley . . . . Taylorsville, Mississippi
Lora Ashley . . . . Taylorsville, Mississippi
Patricia Ashley . . . . Taylorsville, Mississippi
Revecca Goodson . . . . Magee, Mississippi
Maggie Bowen . . . . .Magee, Mississippi
Catyel Griffin . . . . .Laurel, Mississippi
Louis Griffin . . . . Laurel, Mississippi
Terry & Jane PJitts . . . . Laurel, Mississippi
Butch & Rosalie Jones . . . . Moselle, Mississippi
Jack & Barbara Delk .Moselle, Mississippi
Martha Cleveland . . . . Decatur, Mississippi
Lazora Eichelberger .Forest, Mississippi
Melissa Powell . . . . Forest, Mississippi
Janet Richardson . . . . Forest, Mississippi
Carolyn Paremore . . . . .Forest, Mississippi
Neil Hansford . . . . .Tupelo, Mississippi
Ryan Kuklinski . . . . .Eagan, Minnesota
Ashley Reed . . . . Hattiesburg, Mississippi
Beverly Sowell . . . . .Newton, Mississippi
Jim Sowell . . . . .Newton, Mississippi
Jay McCarthy . . . . .Madison, Mississippi
Steve Hardin . . . . Ridgeland, Mississippi
Ken Johnston . . . . .Summit, Mississippi
Roger & Janice Walker . . . . Laurel, Mississippi
Bobie Slay . . . . .Liberty, Mississippi
Brent Kim . . . . .Roswell, Georgia
Sue Sharpliln . . . . .Springhill, Louisiana
Darly Taylor . . . . Canton, Mississippi
Travis Hearst . . . . .Ridgeland, Mississippi
Tina Vincent . . . . Brandon, Mississippi
Terry Day . . . . .Starkville, Mississippi

DAVEY'S CUSTOMERS COME FROM ALL OVER THE WORLD!!!

Carolyn Harry. . . . . Laurel, Mississippi
Louise Burch. . . . . Laurel, Mississippi
Mark Manning. . . . . .Laurel, Mississippi
Sheryl Bostick. . . . . .Austin, Texas
Evelyn Beard. . . . . .Newton, Mississippi
Mark Gilgore. . . . . .Bay Springs, Mississippi
Laura Hope Bishop. . . . . .San Diego, California
Ron Richards. . . . . Orlando, Florida
Gennie & Ray Dursen. . . . . Meridian, Mississippi
Dorthy McDonald. . . . . Bay Springs, Mississippi
Robert & Lovella Watts. . . . . .Raleigh, Mississippi
Terry Bullock. . . . . Hickory, Mississippi
Sherre Hand. . . . . Louin, Mississippi
Bulla Nunnecy. . . . . Laurel, Mississippi
Bay Forntain. Chinquapin, North Carolina
Tim Puckett. . . . . Madison, North Carolina
Vaughn Cowan. . . . . Goldsboro, North Carolina
Rick Manning. . . . . Elizabeth City, North Carolina
Lee Hudgens. . . . . .Greensboro, North Carolina
Barry Harrell. . . . . Kernersville, North Carolina
Marc Holz. . . . . Raleigh, North Carolina
Rob Roakes. . . . . .Salisburg, North Carolina
Jason DeHart. . . . . .Lincolnton, North Carolina
Jeremy Matthews. .Laurel, Mississippi
Kathy Culpepper. . . . . .Bay Springs, Mississippi
Davey Dewitt. . . . . Richton, Mississippi
J. Heil. . . . . Sanderville, Mississippi
Tate Dickey. . . . . .Hattiesburg, Mississippi
Jeanette Graham. . . . . .Ovett, Mississippi
Kristie Lee Shepherd. . . . . Laurel, Mississippi
Melissa M. Terry. . . . . .Laurel, Mississippi
Jerry Terry. . . . . Laurel, Mississippi
Steve Brown. . . . . .Elmore, Alabama
John Taylor. . . . . .Millbrook, Alabama
Melmee Clayton. . . . . Moss Point, Mississippi
John Lowery. . . . . Grand Bay, Alabama
Robert Lowery. . . . . .Moss Point, Mississippi
Sarah Robers. . . . . Collins, Mississippi
Houston McLain. . . . . .Laurel, Mississippi

DAVEY'S CUSTOMERS COME FROM ALL OVER THE WORLD!!!

John C. Steele. Charlotte, North Carolina
Joe Michielsen. Coaldale, Alberta, Canada
Scott Dewitt. . . . . Rock Hill, South Carolina
Darlene Edwards. . . . . Harvey, California
Rev. Kevin Bishop. . . . . Magee, Mississippi
Rev Phillip Hemby . . . . Brookhaven, Mississippi
Judy & Sonny Robbins . . . . Webster, Florida
Mark Singleton . . . . Cherokee, Alabama
Tammy Singleton . . . . Cherokee, Alabama
Steve Reginald . . . . Chillicothe, Illinois
Jeremy Smith . . . . Decatur, Mississippi
Ralph Cahill . . . . Soso, Mississippi
Matt Kinstkey . . . . Copiah, Mississippi
Lon Yeager . . . . Copiah, Mississippi
Charles & Kay Wilcox . . . . Ft. Payne, Alabama
David R. Gaylor . . . . Havana, Florida
Mary & Mark Allen . . . . Wilkes-barre, Pennsylvania
Red Clark . . . . Erin, Tennessee
Connie Brooks . . . . Foley, Alabama
Mary May Rettig . . . . Mobile, Alabama
Cynthia Rettig . . . . Gulf Shores, Alabama
Annie Lou Robinson . . . . Newton, Mississippi
Tommy Robinson . . . . Jackson, Mississippi
Martha Robinson . . . . Jackson, Mississippi
Jeff Miller . . . . Jackson, Mississippi
Tommy Rettig . . . . Slidell, Louisiana
Land Heflin . . . . Missoula, Montana
Erica Johnson . . . . Portland, Oregon
Brian Lewis . . . . Madison, Mississippi
Pat Goforth . . . . Meridian, Mississippi
Johnny Goforth . . . . Meridian, Mississippi
Paul Mann . . . . Meridian, Mississippi
Maudene Heggins . . . . Morton, Mississippi
Evelyn Chain . . . . Daleville, Alabama
Jim & Glynda Corlente . . . . Vossburg, Mississippi
Lyrita Moffett-Parker . . . . Bay Springs, Mississippi
Betty Wilson . . . . Taylorsville, Mississippi
Makitha Page . . . . Louin, Mississippi
Luiz Patena . . . . Waco, Texas
Linda Carol Lewis-Weisinger . . . . Franklin, Kentucky

DAVEY'S CUSTOMERS COME FROM ALL OVER THE WORLD!!!

Minta Vernon . . . . .Franklin, Kentucky
Gwen Heath . . . . .Brandon, Mississippi
Brian Wheaton . . . . Florence, Mississippi
Nettie Procht . . . . Gowanda, New York
Erin Plunkett . . . . Lake, Mississippi
Jaush Russell . . . . Memphis, Tennessee
Ronnie Nichols . . . . .Middleburg, Florida(FEMA)
Randy Meador . . . . .Laurel, Mississippi
Dana Maxwell . . . . .Chunky, Mississippi
Melissa Cahill . . . . Alpharetta, Georgia
Ann Powell . . . . Soso, Mississippi
Allison Maxey . . . . Laurel, Mississippi
Anita McJater . . . . .Soso, Mississippi
Tim Harman . . . . .Mason City, Illinois
Steve Kelly . . . . Decatur, Illinois
Bennie Appleton . . . . .Moulton, Alabama
J. May . . . . Avoco, Iowa
C. Heights . . . . Paxico, Kansas
Keith Gudson . . . . Wamego, Kansas
Bret Eins . . . . Wamego, Kansas
Hugh O'Dale Warren . . . . Tampa, Florida
Louis Lee Davis . . . . .Tampa, Florida
L. C. & Ruth Chaney . . . . Newton, Mississippi
Annie M. Evertt . . . . .Newton, Mississippi
Patricia Baucum . . . . Newton, Mississippi
Tony & Arlie Adams . . . . .Newton, Mississippi
Danny & Brenda Dykes . . . . .Stringer, Mississippi
Debbie Gee . . . . Killen, Alabama
Mark & Donna Marshall . . . . .Las Vegas, Nevada
Marsmar Gussons . . . . Madrid, Spain
Charlotte White . . . . Corpus Christi, Texas
Candi Thillie . . . . Decatur, Mississippi
Dahlia L. Brown . . . . Newton, Mississippi
Lori Gallaspy . . . . .Decatur, Mississippi
Lynne Hasson . . . . Meridian, Mississippi
Berry Lott . . . . .Starkville, Mississippi
July Porswell . . . . .Starkville, Mississippi

DAVEY'S CUSTOMERS COME FROM ALL OVER THE WORLD!!!

Chad Locke . . . . .Madison, Alabama
Buddy Franklin . . . . .Pace, Florida
Don & Kathy Allen . . . . Laurel, Mississippi
Cris Morgan . . . . .Alexandria, Virginia
D. Jalher . . . . .Jonesboro, Arkansas
Jeremy Jones . . . . Jonesboro, Arkansas
Lillian Moody . . . . .Carlisle, Arkansas
Jon Crossett . . . . .Helena, Arkansas
William Surndell .Indianapolis, Indiana
Jim Secrist . . . . Farmville, Virginia
George & Jamie Osborne . . . . .San Antonio, Texas
Carole Hester . . . . .Stringer, Mississippi
Kenneth Loch . . . . .Dallas, Georgia
Jeremy Smith . . . . Dalton, Georgia
Terry Williams . . . . .Trion, Georgia
Max & Suzi Phillips . . . . Taylorsville, Mississippi
John Riffe . . . . Rockville, Indiana
Dewey Gregory . . . . Flippin, Arkansas
Williams Folkes . . . . .Hattiesburg, Mississippi
Elizabeth Lofton . . . . .Clinton, Mississippi
Katie Folkes . . . . Hattiesburg, Mississippi
Charlie Lavender . . . . .Madden, Mississippi
Nic Norton . . . . Sidney, Nebraska
Barbara Ray . . . . .Jacksonville, Florida
Brian Merchant . . . . .Jacksonville, Florida
Eddie Davis . . . . Locust Grove, Georgia
Belinda Grainger . . . . Panama City, Florida
Monique Langlais . . . . .France
Lanithin Hardaway . . . . Laurel, Mississippi
Vince Hardaway . . . . Laurel, Mississippi
Mike Voegele . . . . Minneapolis, Minnesota
Kirby Horton . . . . .Nashville, Tennessee
Mike Tompkins . . . . Winona, Mississippi
Clay Brown . . . . Mendenhall, Mississippi
Bill Yawn . . . . .Petal, Mississippi
Linda & Ed Breland . . . . .Laurel, Mississippi
Jon Welborn . . . . Laurel, Mississippi
Ruth Morris . . . . Louisville, Kentucky
Charlie Pate . . . . .Carrollton, Alabama

DAVEY'S CUSTOMERS COME FROM ALL OVER THE WORLD!!!

Jerry Pate . . . . Carrollton, Alabama
Ed & Donna Evan . . . . Lake, Mississippi
Lorrie & Dan Landrum . . . . Laurel, Mississippi
Ridgeland Jones . . . . Laurel, Mississippi
Mike Brown . . . . Mendenhall, Mississippi
Tim Smith . . . . Bay Springs, Mississippi
Mario Gastelum . . . . San Diego, California
Gina Ravenhorst . . . . Sumrall, Mississippi
Franklin Silves . . . . Macon, Mississippi
Mary Williams . . . . Macon, Mississippi
Lae Heard . . . . Brooksville, Mississippi
Renee Strickland . . . . Bay Springs, Mississippi
Randy Brewer . . . . Jackson, Mississippi
Susan Mint . . . . Hattiesburg, Mississippi
Chad Stringer . . . . Canrel, Mississippi
Al Rossi . . . . Bakersfield, California
Billie Ulmer . . . . Rose Hill, Mississippi
John Harper . . . . Laurel, Mississippi
Marie Miro . . . . Los Angeles, California
Tiggan Keshishyan . . . . Los Angeles, California
Bert Craft . . . . Gordo, Alabama
Chad Gilreath . . . . Fayette, Alabama
Willis O. Lofton . . . . Tucson, Arizona
Chuck Broadus . . . . Ocean Springs, Mississippi
Chris Rubom . . . . Hurley, Mississippi
Mike Mattson . . . . Fargo, North Dakota
Jim & Mary Seay . . . . Pasco, Washington
Thomas & George Spradley . . . . Laurel, Mississippi
Roy Spradley . . . . Laurel, Mississippi
Tubby & Linda Clark . . . . Laurel, Mississippi
Stevie & Nancy . . . . Laurel, Mississippi
Barry & Cheryl Rewer . . . . Laurel, Mississippi
Mario & Alicia Genna . . . . Stringer, Mississippi
Lee & Karen Matthews . . . . Laurel, Mississippi
Keith & Brenda Rogers . . . . Laurel, Mississippi
Donald & Gay Pounders
Janson Bounds . . . . Hattiesburg, Mississippi
C. Tadlock . . . . Forest, Mississippi
David Tadlock . . . . Forest, Mississippi

200

DAVEY'S CUSTOMERS COME FROM ALL OVER THE WORLD!!!

Sandy Tadlock . . . . Forest, Mississippi
G. Tadlock . . . . Forest, Mississippi
Trent Travis . . . . Forest, Mississippi
Corbin Hurst . . . . Hickory, Mississippi
Colton Hurst . . . . Hickory, Mississippi
Sidney Stevens . . . . College Station, Texas
Jennie Stevens . . . . Gulfport, Mississippi
Bobby Arruthers . . . . Jackson, Mississippi
Ray Watts . . . . Jackson, Mississippi
Dezaree Jenkins . . . . Locust Grove, Georgia
Chad Davis . . . . Locust Grove, Georgia
Judy Conn . . . . Hattiesburg, Mississippi
Shirley Parker . . . . Milton, Florida
Debbi Smith . . . . The Woodlands, Texas
Bill Smith . . . . The Woodlands, Texas
Rich Rahaim . . . . Heidelberg, Mississippi
Austin Bishop . . . . Meridian, Mississippi
John Richardson . . . . Madison, Mississippi
William Richardson . . . . Forest, Mississippi
H. L. Richard . . . . Forest, Mississippi
Linda Brune . . . . Ridgeland, Mississippi
Merlene Chandler . . . . Stringer, Mississippi
Jimmy Chandler Jr. . . . . Laurel, Mississippi
Roscoe Besson, Jr. . . . . Galliano, Louisiana
Loui Besson . . . . Galliano, Louisiana
Sidni Page . . . . Galliano, Louisiana
Kelly & Martiel Bullock . . . . Laurel, Mississippi
Raymond Kell . . . . Stone Mountain, Georgia
Mary Buchanan . . . . Soso, Mississippi
Ronald Buchanan . . . . Laurel, Mississippi
Wilson Sistrunk . . . . Magee, Mississippi
BRO. James Sistrunk . . . . Mt. Olive, Mississippi
Virginia Shumaker . . . . Mt. Olive, Mississippi
Angela Curtis . . . . Pensacola, Florida
Rick Howie . . . . Pensacola, Florida
Samson Norman . . . . Bay Springs, Mississippi
Jean Chandler . . . . Toomsuba, Mississippi
Stanley Walsh . . . . Newton, Mississippi
Will Petterson . . . . Meridian, Mississippi

DAVEY'S CUSTOMERS COME FROM ALL OVER THE WORLD!!!

Tom & Dee Dee Glaze .... Polkville, Mississippi
Jerry & Vanessa Bennett .... Columbus, OH/ Winfield, WV
Janice Rowell ....Laurel, Mississippi
Jerry Kirk .... Laurel, Mississippi
Mark Valenteno .... Ridgeland, Mississippi
Jerry May .... Little Rock, Mississippi
Ronald Read ....Raleigh, Mississippi
Mark Sullivan .... Laurel, Mississippi
Blue & Jan Barnes ....Wilsonville, Alabama
Joe & Deloris Booth ....
Renee Gilbert .... Hattiesburg, Mississippi
Lacy Lott ....Purvis, Mississippi
Adrain Jordan .... Ft. Worth, Texas
Shelby Lynn Jordan .... Ft. Worth, Texas
Judge Billy G. Bridges ....Brandon, Mississippi
Coy & Jennifer Deaton .... Rome, Georgia
Greg Deaton .... Rome, Georgia
Clay & Morgony Waggood ....Anchorage, Arkansas
Ron & Beth Balis ....Hattiesburg, Mississippi
Patrick Boyd ....Corinth, Mississippi
Rick Smith ....
Danny Mabry .... Butler, Alabama
Daniel Mabry .... Meridian, Mississippi
Andy Boutwell ....Butler, Alabama
Bobbie Butler ....Taylorsville, Mississippi
Ray Aycock ....Jackson, Mississippi
Gil Ray ....Jackson, Mississippi
Rob Guerriero ....Jackson, Mississippi
Ed Morgan .... Brookhaven, Mississippi
Josie Smith .... Prentiss, Mississippi
Ralph Smith, III ....Prentiss, Mississippi
Doug Hill ....Jasper Co. Sheriff Dept.
Chris McCullouh ....Jasper Co. Sheriff Dept.
Kenneth & Fran Beard .... Enterprise, Mississippi
David L. Hagan .... .Laurel, Mississippi
Ramona Walters .... Stringer, Mississippi
Melissa Buckley .... .Stringer, Mississippi
Al Shoemaker ....Laurel, Mississippi
Perry Taylor ....Laurel, Mississippi

DAVEY'S CUSTOMERS COME FROM ALL OVER THE WORLD!!!

Shelley Boone . . . . .Meridian, Mississippi
Lenney C. . . . . New Orleans, Louisiana
Ginger Burks . . . . .Hattiesburg, Mississippi
Alley Bridges . . . . Richton, Mississippi
Chad Bridges . . . . .Richton, Mississippi
Lana Myers . . . . Laurel, Mississippi
Debra Tisdale . . . . Laurel, Mississippi
Debbie Morris . . . . .Laurel, Mississippi
Jennifer Windham . . . . Beaumont, Mississippi
Don & Linda Brewer . . . . .St. Simons Island, Georgia
Tommy Ray & Andre Wall . . . . Newton, Mississippi
James & Becky Shutt . . . . Savannah, Tennessee
Larry Wilson . . . . .Murresboro, Tennessee
Harry Ladner . . . . Pass Christian, Mississippi
Melisia Pelham . . . . Laurel, Mississippi
Stephen Rice . . . . Shreveport, Louisiana
Matthew Anglin . . . . Ovett, Mississippi
Greg Tarpley . . . . .Anderson, Alabama
Ray Plaf . . . . .Jacksonville, Florida
Trenton Bates . . . . .Wheatcroft, Kentucky
Charles Lee . . . . .Gainesville, Georgia
Jimmy Filmore . . . . .Collinsville, Alabama
Chris Flemming .Rogersville, Alabama
Sean Kelly . . . . Zimbabwe, Africa
Jeffery Roninson . . . . Orange, Texas
Craig Robinson . . . . .Mauriceville
Brad Steuck . . . . Hume, Missouri
Mario & Maribel Yanes . . . . Hidalgo, Mexico
Wayne & Diane Mims . . . . .Bay Springs, Mississippi
R.E. & Mrs. George Snitbar . . . . .Newton, Mississippi
Carl & Catt Ivey .Taylorsville, Mississippi
Myrtle L. Ellis . . . . .Newton, Mississippi
Bea Williamson . . . . Meridian, Mississippi
Frances Robinson . . . . Meridian, Mississippi
Kathleen Semmes . . . . Meridian, Mississippi
Ray Flemming . . . . .Philadelphia, Mississippi
Kathy King . . . . .Meridian, Mississippi
John Northcutt . . . . Hattiesburg, Mississippi
Micah Raymond . . . . .Grandview, Washington

DAVEY'S CUSTOMERS COME FROM ALL OVER THE WORLD!!!

Met & Charles Stennis . . . . Meridian, Mississippi
Veronica Terrell. Meridian, Mississippi
Chuck Kolen. . . . . .Bettendorf, Indiana
Donny Smith. . . . . Blooming Prairie, Minnesota
Ryan Sandhaus. . . . . Tallahassee, Florida
Melinda Carter. . . . . .Chnehatta, Mississippi
Doug Massey. . . . . .Newton, Mississippi
Vanessa Shepherd. . . . . .Bay Springs, Mississippi
C. J. Westbrook. Sylvarena, Mississippi
Rex Grant. . . . . .Crossett, Arkansas
Sharon Grant . . . . .Crossett, Arkansas
Jean Westbrook . . . . .Raleigh, Mississippi
Ricky Breakfield . . . . Columbia, Mississippi
April Thatch . . . . .Heidelberg, Mississippi
Angela Tisdale . . . . Ellisville, Mississippi
Ron Taylor . . . . Laurel, Mississippi
Stephaine Thornton . . . . .Laurel, Mississippi
Judi McQueen . . . . .Laurel, Mississippi
Brian Bunnell . . . . .Richton, Mississippi
Lavon Evans . . . . .Laurel, Mississippi
Peggy Keyes . . . . Hattiesburg, Mississippi
Wilma C. Stroo . . . . Hattiesburg, Mississippi
Brent Parne . . . . Laurel, Mississippi
Cindy Pittman . . . . Laurel, Mississippi
Holley Lacey . . . . .Laurel, Mississippi
Nancy Allen . . . . Laurel, Mississippi
Sandra, Greg, Ambrea & Patrick Lane . . . . .Meridian, Mississippi
Joe Parker . . . . .Sandersville, Mississippi
Norma Herrington . . . . .Laurel, Mississippi
Martyn & Marcia Ballestero . . . . .South Bend, Indiana
Bettie Jo Rakes . . . . .Newton, Mississippi
Tyler Norman . . . . Newton, Mississippi
Rose Mary Alford .Newton, Mississippi
Glenn Ruffin Green . . . . Louin, Mississippi
Boyce Christopher . . . . .Madison, Mississippi
Michael Martin . . . . .Madison, Mississippi
Paul G. McKay . . . . Biloxi, Mississippi

DAVEY'S CUSTOMERS COME FROM ALL OVER THE WORLD!!!

Chris Harris	Hillsboro, Mississippi
Gaylon Bradshaw	Nt. Nebo, Mississippi
Glynn & Sandra Rea	Moss Point, Mississippi
Jeremy, Jennifer, & Austin Brown	
Bethany Brown	Mendenhall, Mississippi
Glenn Parker	Florida
Danny & Veronica Hamm	Laurel, Mississippi
Clint Myers	Laurel, Mississippi
Cecil Myers	Laurel, Mississippi
Allen Muse	Union, Mississippi
Sheryl Hensel	Meridian, Mississippi
Dianna Breland	Union, Mississippi
Dale Boler	Union, Mississippi
Faye & Darla Loftis	Union, Mississippi
Jerry Cranmore	
Mary Jo Chanaud	Centreville, Maryland
Harold & Clara Hughes	New Orleans, Louisiana
Kevin Rhodes	Pelahatchie, Mississippi
Kurt Rhodes	Pelahatchie, Mississippi
Kyle Rhodes	Pelahatchie, Mississippi
Tim Morgan	Flowery Branch, Georgia
Skip Smith	Forest City, North Carolina
James & Ada Mooney	Philadelphia, Mississippi
Marty & Michelle Cowden	Brandon, Mississippi
Polly Cowden	Brandon, Mississippi
Robbie & Jack Herrington	Bay Springs, Mississippi
Ed & Joyce Smith	Laurel, Mississippi
Ida Ruth C. Smith	Moss Point, Mississippi
Idam Chapman	Moss Point, Mississippi
Cliff Currie	Raleigh, Mississippi
Shirley Bonnett	Eros, Louisiana
Buddy Bonnett	Eros, Louisiana
Gordon Malone	Albin, Wyoming
Tim R. Ishee	Laurel, Mississippi
David Summers	Rayville, Louisiana
Bennie C Goudy, Jr.	Meridian, Mississippi
Paul Morris	Louin, Mississippi
Hubert & Wanda Graver	Philadephia, Mississippi

DAVEY'S CUSTOMERS COME FROM ALL OVER THE WORLD!!!

Chad Hurla . . . . McFarland, Kansas
Barbara Ray . . . . Jacksonville, Florida
Annie Wilson . . . . Jacksonville, Florida
Tina Wilson . . . . Jacksonville, Florida
Bryce Frye . . . . Jacksonville, Florida
Scott Buffington . . . . Collins, Mississippi
A. D. Buffington . . . . Flowood, Mississippi
Shirley Parker . . . . Milton, Florida
Frances Kennedy . . . . Highland, California
Patrick Lane . . . . Meridian, Mississippi
Ricky & Rusty Wasoom . . . . Greensburg, Louisiana
Cynthai Morris . . . . Reno, Nevada
Shirley Jean Johnson . . . . Union, Mississippi
Buddy & Betty Flavas . . . . Laurel, Mississippi
Millie & Jack McCraw . . . . Laurel, Mississippi
Mary Kathryn Abercrombie . . . . Soso, Mississippi
Dot Turner . . . . Soso, Mississippi
Dorothy Barr . . . . Laurel, Mississippi
Eva Cheeks . . . . Soso, Mississippi
Viviav Cheeks . . . . Ellisville, Mississippi
Tim Walsh . . . . Oxford, Mississippi
Kristin Livingston . . . . Manton, Michigan
Lori Giovengo . . . . Laurel, Mississippi
Cynthai Rahaim . . . . Heidelberg, Mississippi
Jan Blake . . . . Laurel, Mississippi
Jason & Dora Willoughby . . . . Queens, New York
Brooke Griffith . . . . Hickory, Mississippi
Marva Cavenaugh . . . . Meridian, Mississippi
Barbara E. Hawks . . . . Memphis, Tennessee
George Everett . . . . Meridian, Mississippi
Debbbie Coghlan . . . . Newton, Mississippi
Karen Fleming . . . . Newton, Mississippi
Brad Grantham . . . . Newton, Mississippi
Ben Blackwell . . . . Brandon, Mississippi
Jimmie D. Pickering . . . . Jackson, Mississippi
Eric Bounds . . . . Atlanta, Georgia
Rebekah Rettig-Turner . . . . Seattle, Washington
Cynthia Retig . . . . Gulf Shores, Alabama
Connie S. . . . . Gulf Shores, Alabama

DAVEY'S CUSTOMERS COME FROM ALL OVER THE WORLD!!!

Dickie Dixon . . . .

Arland & Rose Heidelberg. . . . .

Danny William. . . . .

Betty Michael. . . . . .Rienzi, Mississippi

Sherrie & Chuck Thompson . . . . Amite, Louisiana

REP. Lee Jarrel Davis . . . . .Hattiesburg, Mississippi

Paul Dawson . . . . Dacula, Georgia

Harvey Reeves . . . . Amory, Mississippi

Dale Olsen . . . . .Russellville, Arkansas

Sharon Howard . . . .

Alan Williams . . . . .Hattiesburg, Mississippi

Brittany Blacklidge . . . . Gulfport, Mississippi

Michelle Blacklidge . . . . .Gulfport, Mississippi

Virginia Simmons . . . . Newton, Mississippi

Andy Kolp . . . . Fond du Lac, Wisconsin

Tom Benedict .Fond du Lac, Wisconsin

Elsie Manouw . . . . Fond du Lac, Wisconsin

Kenneth (Fire Truck) Jones . . . .

Danielle S. Garrison, DVM, ...Bay Springs, Mississippi

David Garrison . . . . .Bay Springs, Mississippi

Phillip Stanley . . . .

P. Sullivan . . . .

Keith Richoux . . . . .Mandeville, Louisiana

Allan & Sandra Jones . . . . Hickory, Mississippi

Clint Wright . . . . Union, Mississippi

Christopher Harrelson . . . . Forest, Mississippi

David Jones .Walnut Grove, Mississippi

Nicholas & Quinteena Dardar . . . . Mize, Mississippi

Kathryn H Hutton . . . . Jackson, Mississippi

Mary Ann Marray . . . . Taylorsville, Mississippi

Ynonne Murray . . . . .Jackson, Mississippi

Roger Feiertag . . . . .Decatur, Illinios

Nishant Bhatt Ahmedabad Gujarat . . . . .India/ Decatur,Il

Ilgreg Glowski . . . . .Decatur, Illinios

Ronnie Backllidge, Jr. . . . . .Gulfport, Mississippi

Julie Sharp . . . . Meridian, Mississippi

Ann Craven . . . . Meridian, Mississippi

Pat Elam . . . . .Meridian, Mississippi

Patricia B. Holt . . . . Meridian, Mississippi

DAVEY'S CUSTOMERS COME FROM ALL OVER THE WORLD!!!

Susie Broadhead. . . . . .Merdian, Mississippi
Jack Winstead. . . . . Lawrence,Mississippi
Glenn Lowell. . . . . Newton, Mississippi
Kelly Wells. . . . . .Brandon, Mississippi
Adam Harlins. . . . . Logandale, Nevada
Chris Martinez. . . . . Baton Rouge, Louisiana
Jeff Watkins. . . . . Forest, Mississippi
Terry & Patricck McKelvey. . . . . .Little Rock, Arkansas
Phil & Debbie Kitchens. Soso, Mississppi
Tomare Dyvzek. . . . . .Swidnica, Poland
Mike Brown. . . . . D'lo, Mississippi
Lester Scott. . . . . Laurel, Mississippi
Job Michael. . . . . .Jackson, California
Brian Michael. . . . . .San Jose, California
Darryl Michael. . . . . .Belmont, California
Pat & Bob Michael. . . . .
E. Michael. . . . .
Brandi Calliso. . . . . Laurel, Mississippi
Hanh Washaven. . . . . Northern California
Khalid Abdou . . . . Sudan, Africa/Decatur, Illinios
Shawn L. Mitchell . . . . .Decatur, Illinios
Bob Hand . . . . Decatur, Illinios
Leanne Bartholet . . . . Akron, Ohio
Marti Reece . . . . Pine Bluff, Arkansas
Maxine & Lonnie Wheller . . . . Heidelberg, Mississippi
Tom Butler . . . . Meridian, Mississippi
Sen. V. Cawhal. . . . .
Lovy Rush. . . . .
Patsy Carey. . . . . .Union, Mississippi
Belinda Pitts Harrison . . . . Laurel, Mississippi
Butch Red III. . . . .
Marcus & Ronda Gully . . . . Bay Springs, Mississippi
Elizabeth Dees. . . . .
Kathy & Bobby White. . . . .
Rena & Howard Hilton. . . . . Taylorsville, Mississippi
Benny Carter. . . . . Meridian, Mississippi
Amy Woodward . . . . Starkville, Mississippi
Gloria & Richard Brown. . . . . .Oklahoma City, Oklahoma
Tony & Lisa Breazeale. . . . . .Laurel, Mississippi

DAVEY'S CUSTOMERS COME FROM ALL OVER THE WORLD!!!

Michale Herring . . . .
Phil Campbell . . . . .Alabama
Bobby Slater . . . . Waldron, Arkansas
Jo Bender . . . . Laurel, Mississippi
Margie Bonner . . . . .Heidelberg, Mississippi
Jimmy Dyess . . . .
Kerry McDonald . . . . .Ft. Worth, Texas
Laren*Volarvich . . . . .Decatur, Mississippi
Debbie Laird . . . . .Lake, Mississippi
Wyatt & Faye Malbel .Ellisville, Mississippi
Jim& Carole Kelly . . . . .Ellisville, Mississippi
Gary Ross . . . . Los Angeles, California
Diane Alvarez . . . . Los Angeles, California
Robin Bissell . . . . .Los Angeles, California
Elsie Gavin McGill White . . . . New Orleans, Louisiana
Marvin Davis . . . . .Chicago, Illinois
Jason Pickens . . . . .Chicago, Illinois
Dell Washington . . . . .Jasper County
Orie Ratcliff . . . .
Daniel & Amy Wood .Laurel, Mississippi
Cecil Harper . . . . Soso, Mississippi
Jim Ishee . . . . Vidor, Texas
Rich Glamann . . . . Grand Island, Nebraska
Jason Bush . . . . .Brandon, Mississippi
M. B. Stringer, Jr. . . . . Collierville, Tennessee
Jo Nell Stringer . . . . .Bay Springs, Mississippi
Diana Smigij . . . . .Selah, Washington
Jean Porter . . . . .Selah, Washington
Bobbie Reinko . . . . Richmond, Texas
Traci Smith . . . . Richmond, Texas
Vicki Stevens . . . . .College Station, Texas
Bobby & Ann Craven . . . . Meridian, Mississippi
Shane & Kim Craven . . . . Gainesville, Florida
Pre Kaya Carter . . . . .Aurora, Colorado
Nick Hillman . . . . Taylorsville, Mississippi
Wesley Hall . . . .
Albet Kennedy . . . .
Monte Gagon Ceilo . . . . Gordo, Illinois
Scott Pond . . . . Central, Illinois

DAVEY'S CUSTOMERS COME FROM ALL OVER THE WORLD!!!

Hill & Christie Graham. . . . .

Billy Ray Thompson. . . . . .Chicago, Illinois

Tracy Parker. . . . .

Mike Stringer. . . . .

Terry Green. . . . .

Chester Dayvolt . . . .

Chad Wiggs. . . . .

Allen Quin . . . .

Matilde . . . . Spain

Griff Samon. . . . . .Brandon, Mississippi

Eddie. . . . . .Ridgeland, Mississippi

Nathaniel & Helen Nickey. . . . .

Drew Troxler. . . . . Brandon, Mississippi

Ken Sharp. . . . . .Charleston, South Carolina

Steve Carmody. . . . . ,. . . .Jackson Mississippi

Art Felix. . . . . .Baldwin Park, California

Thomas Laing. . . . . .Hixson, Tennessee

Bill Laing. . . . . .Memphis, Tennessee

Mike & Shirley Collins. . . . . .Culver City, California

Amber Haun. . . . . .Decatur, Illinois

Dave Barr. . . . . Decator Illinois

Norma Jones. . . . . .Columbia, Mississippi

Dorothy McCormick. . . . . Turnerville, Mississippi

Libby Parker. . . . . Louin, Misisippi

Ann James. . . . . Louin Mississippi

Tate James. . . . . .Bay Springs, Mississippi

Jane Pritchett. . . . . .Louin, Mississippi

Joel W. Jefcoat. . . . . .Soso, Mississippi

Joel McClellan. . . . . .Mize, Mississippi

David W. Knight. . . . . Louin, Mississippi

Seth "The Bear" Ellzey. . . . . .Semme, Alabama

Charlie Ellzey . . . . .Keysville, Georgia

Eva Cheeks. . . . . .Soso, Mississippi

Bob Mari. . . . . Decatur, Illinois

Felicia Tayamen. . . . . .Garland, Texas

Priscilla & Lowell Stivison. Monticello, Arkansas

DAVEY'S CUSTOMERS COME FROM ALL OVER THE WORLD!!!

Yvonne Thigpen. . . . . Jackson, Mississippi
Greg Charney. . . . . Houston, Texas
Beau, Gena & Brad Broadus. . . . . Calico Rock, Arkansas
Luke Howard . . . . Millington, Maryland
Marlin Hurst. . . . . New Holland, Pennsylvania
Dave Burkholder . . . . Chambersburg, Pennsylvania
Leroy Strite . . . . Bay Springs, Mississippi
Larry G. Strite. . . . . .Chambersburg, Pennsylvania
Mike Balog. . . . . Ontario, Canada
Sue Varisocker. . . . . Monroe, Michigan
Dennis Poland. . . . . Spring City, Tennessee
Dick Beteran. . . . . Temperance, Michigan
Dan Gibson. . . . . Crystal Springs, Mississippi
Sylvia Rolison. . . . .
Monica Kelley. . . . .
Lola Gavin Brown. . . . . Bay Springs, Mississippi
Deanna Green . . . . Salt Lake City, Utah
Carolyn Bass. . . . . Salt Lake City, Utah
Alazar Cesar Andrade. . . . . Sorocaba, Brazil
LaDawn Griffin. . . . . Memphis, Tennessee
Don Sims . . . . Atlanta, Georgia
Kevin Stump. . . . . Springfield, Illinois
Ted Johnson. . . . . Lake, Mississippi
Sandie Johnson. . . . . .Lake, Mississippi
Randy & Donna Corley . . . . Bay Springs, Mississippi
Dewitt Reed. . . . . .Heidelberg, Mississippi
Anita Guinn. . . . . Maxie, Mississippi
Joseph A. Larry. . . . . Jackson, Mississippi
Larry Catlin. . . . . .Bryan, Texas
Wally Walden. . . . . Mobile,Alabama
Eileen Rocconi . . . . Cleveland, Mississippi
Jennifer McAdary . . . . Louisville, Mississippi
Carol McAdory . . . . Noxapater, Mississippi
Bruce & Linda Kirk . . . . .Noxapater, Mississippi
Vaughn & Melinda Byrd . . . . Mize, Mississippi
Issac K. Byrd . . . . Jackson, Mississippi

DAVEY'S CUSTOMERS COME FROM ALL OVER THE WORLD!!!

Bobby S. Alford . . . .

Kathy Spire . . . . .Union, Mississippi

Becky Granning . . . . .Union, Mississippi

Tony Landry . . . . .Brandon, Mississippi

Lexi, Alli, & Layton Landry . . . . .Brandon, Mississippi

Kim Landry . . . . .Brandon, Mississippi

Skip Scaggs . . . . .Meridian

Sarah Roland . . . . .Shannon, Mississippi

Bobbie & Rusty Burwell . . . . .South Orange, New Jersey

Greig Thibodeaux . . . . .Harvey, Louisiana

Pete & Janep Canigaro . . . . .Brandon, Mississippi

Brad Munvea . . . . .Locust Grove, California

Eddie Davis . . . . .Locust Grove, California

Tom Boyko . . . . .Ocoee, Florida

Kendal Jolly . . . . .Orlando, Florida

Gloria Jolly . . . . .Russell, Mississippi

Kathy Hinshaw . . . . .Laurel, Mississippi

Corey O. Hinshaw .Jackson, Mississippi

Charlie Mars . . . . .Oxford, Mississippi

Lindsey Brown . . . . .Meridian, Mississippi

Haskel & Wanda Rogers . . . . .Kingwood, Texas

Burma Dale Harris . . . . .Bay Springs

Charles Rogers . . . . .Bay Springs

Roger Harrison . . . . .Beulah Hubbard

Jeffery Harrison . . . . .Beulah Hubbard

Molley Childress . . . . .Laurel, Mississippi

Carson Humphries . . . . .Durant, Mississippi

David & Mary Childres . . . . .Laurel, Mississippi

Mr. & Mrs. Bill Graves . . . . .McComb, Mississippi

Myrl Bowen . . . . .McComb, Mississippi

Ken & Rhonda Murray . . . . .McComb, Mississippi

Paul G. McKay . . . . .Biloxi, Mississippi

Becky Tyree . . . . .Meridian, Mississippi

Sonny Nettles . . . . .Louin, Mississippi

Jo Ann Moore . . . . .Petal, Mississippi

DAVEY'S CUSTOMERS COME FROM ALL OVER THE WORLD!!!

Steve Yon . . . . *Biloxi, Mississippi*

Alex & Amanda White . . . . *Charleston, South Carolina*

William Scott Mathemy . . . . *Laurel, Mississippi*

J. Malcolm Henderson . . . . *Laurel, Mississippi*

Rebekah Garrison . . . . *Summerland, Mississippi*

Bri Williams . . . . *Meridian, Mississippi*

Scott & Alice Cash . . . . *Laurel, Mississippi*

Merle & Norman Von Wettberg . . . . *Hamilton, New York*

Bobby Perrebonne . . . .

Berggie Vegas . . . . *Grand Isle, California*

Barbara Dabdoub . . . . *Meridian, Mississippi*

Lauran Anderson . . . . *Petal, Mississippi*

Kylie Harrell . . . . *Petal, Mississippi*

Lisa Fairchild . . . . *Myrtle Creek, Oregon*

Norman Patry . . . . *Cope Elizabeth, Maine*

Mark Shaheen . . . . *Minneapolis, Minnesota*

Jim Barloxy . . . . *Joliet, Illinois*

Laurent Deconinck . . . . *Belgium, Europe*

Randolo B. Cuttino . . . . *Georgetown, South Carolina*

Imdad U. Sheikh . . . . *Jasper, Indiana*

Jimmy & Renee Tillman . . . . *Philadelphia, Mississippi*

Jim Kelly (Free State of Jones) . . . . *Ellisville, Mississippi*

Caroline Kelly . . . . *Ellisville, Mississippi*

Frank Marshall . . . . *Pacific Palisades, California*

Kathleen Kennedy . . . . *Pacific Palisades, California*

Gavy Ross . . . . *Los Angeles, California*

Robin Bissell . . . . *Los Angeles, California*

Faye Moulds . . . . *Ellisville, Mississippi*

Wyatt Moulds . . . . *Ellisville, Mississippi*

J. Vincent Douglas . . . . *Greenville, South Carolina*

Rev. Arehit Holley . . . . *Escataupa, Mississippi*

Thomas A. Osborne . . . . *Moss Point, Mississippi*

Don Macke . . . . *Lincoln, Nebraska*

Tommy Aclon . . . . *Meridian, Mississippi*

Wayne Westbrook . . . . *Newton, Mississippi*

DAVEY'S CUSTOMERS COME FROM ALL OVER THE WORLD!!!

Bobby Matchener ....Brandon, Mississippi

Janise Cranford ....Abbeville, Louisiana

Marcus Boyles ....Waynesboro, Mississippi

Thomas Ruffin ....Ellisville, Mississippi

Jim Kelley ....Ellisville, Mississippi

Keith Shelby (Jasper CMEI) ....Moss, Mississippi

Charles Gergeni ....Clayton, Georgia

Andrea Williams ....WTOK-TV, Meridian

Sidney Luvene ....WTOK-TV, Meridian

Wayne Kuiken ....N. Haledon, New Jersey

Betty Kuiken ....N. Haledon, New Jersey

Beth Stevens ....Mt. Olive, Mississippi

Dora A. Garbner ....Mt. Olive, Mississippi

Joe Garbner ....Mt. Olive, Mississippi

Norman Stevens ....Mt. Olive, Mississippi

Rev. Michael A Distell ....West Monroe, Louisiana

William A. Distell ....West Monroe, Louisiana

Matthew Windham ....Ras, Mississippi

Betty McNab ....Valparaiso, Florida

Sallie McDavis "Great Food!" ....Dallas, Texas

Candace Whitentar ....Dauphin Island, Alabama

Calvace & Nell Luckett ....Joliet, Illinois

Mike Pittman ....Corinth, Mississippi

Fulton Pittman ....Cory, North Carolina

Thomas Rauiponi ....Italy

Patrick Jott ....High Point, North Carolina

Bud Caywood ....Taylorsville, North Carolina

Kevin Rigdon ....Union, Mississippi

Jeff Taylor ....Union, Mississippi

Charles W. Johnson ....Ellisville, Mississippi

Jac Lentz "Might Fine Food" ....Brighton, Michigan

Jeremy Robichaux ....Rayne, Louisiana

William Scott ....Winnsboro, Louisiana

Don Gilbert ....Forest, Mississippi

DAVEY'S CUSTOMERS COME FROM ALL OVER THE WORLD!!!

Dot Strickling . . . . .Oxford, Mississippi
Mr. & Mrs. Clayton Blount . . . . .Decatur, Mississippi
Talitha Speed . . . . .Forest, Mississippi
Brad Hammons . . . . .Pineville, Mississippi
Frankie Hammone . . . . .Pineville, Mississippi
Jeremy Calhoun . . . . .Monticello, Arkansas
Jonathan McDoughald . . . . .Warren, Arkansas
W. Hastings . . . . .Laurel, Mississippi
Don Norman . . . . .Laurel, Mississippi
Glen Tillman . . . .
Bob & Margaret Rayburn . . . . .Laurel, Mississippi
Debbie Farrish . . . . .Ellisville, Mississippi
Alice & Breland Dolison . . . . .Ellisville, Mississippi
Bonnie Foley . . . . .Stringer, Mississippi
Cheryl Lutsch . . . . .Wooster, Ohio
Cliv Dore . . . . .Perry, Maine
Simon Parrish . . . . .Norwich, England
John Perdue . . . . .Durham, Maine
Malcolm Parrish . . . . .England
Cathy Thompson . . . . .Morton, Mississippi
Tammy Wesson . . . . .Brandon, Mississippi
Rick Guy . . . . .Pachuta, Mississippi
Will Ball . . . . .Nanih Waiya, Mississippi
Wynell Simmons .Zachery, Louisiana
Emily LeBlanc . . . . .Zachary, Louisiana
Helene & Arthur Erickson . . . . .Big Bear Lake, California
Charlie & Brenda Embrey . . . . .Hickory, Mississippi
Larry & Janice Erickson . . . . .Big Bear Lake, California
Alfred & Anna-Mari Embrey . . . . .Orange, California
Diane Chilton . . . . .Frazee, Minnesota
Margaret Stauburl . . . . .Bayley, Minnesota
Denise Wilson . . . . .Frazee, Minnesota
Liz Barlow . . . . .Laurel, Mississippi
Alice Kelley . . . . .Laurel, Mississippi
Leon & Glenda Lewis . . . . .Gulfport, Mississippi

DAVEY'S CUSTOMERS COME FROM ALL OVER THE WORLD!!!

Doris Richardson . . . .*Newton, Mississippi*

Teddy & Darlene Goodwin . . . .*DeWitt, Nebraska*

Kirsti Grodahl . . . .*Minneapolis, Minnesota*

Patsy Stringer . . . .*Bloomington, Minnesota*

Charles Murphrey . . . .*Birmingham, Alabama*

Percy Pearson . . . .*Decatur, Mississippi*

Rodney Toler . . . .*Meridian, Mississippi*

Bob Lindsey . . . .*Newton, Mississippi*

Glenda Baucum . . . .*Newton, Mississippi*

Addie Sue Mardis . . . .*New Augusta, Mississippi*

Carolyn McCardle . . . .*New Augusta, Mississippi*

Mr. & Mrs. Wendy Wagner . . . .*Malden, Mississippi*

Mr. & Mrs. Samuel E. Clemons . . . .*Gautier, Mississippi*

Carol Bennett . . . .*Brooklyn, New York*

James Clemons . . . .*Pascagoula, Mississippi*

Billy Shimp . . . .*Brooklyn, Mississippi*

Virginia Rigley . . . .*Brooklyn, Mississippi*

Randy Miller . . . .*Evensville, Tennessee*

Allen Grogan . . . .*Spring City, Tennessee*

Boot DuPre-Milner . . . .*Siloam Springs, Arkansas*

Celeste Harris . . . .*Birmingham, Alabama*

Jim Pigott . . . .*Gluckstadt, Mississippi*

Dick Minbauer . . . .*Apache Junction, Arizona*

Adi McGray . . . .*Newton, Mississippi*

Dick Peterson . . . .*Temperance, Minnesota*

Dave Piacenti . . . .*Ferrysburg, Ohio*

Eric Hulsemann . . . .*Monroe, Minnesota*

Jarvis L. . . . .*Monroe, Minnesota*

Dale M. . . . .*Monroe, Minnesota*

Frances C. Wilson . . . . ,.*Newton, Mississippi*

Peggy Gaines . . . .*Newton, Mississippi*

Lexy Clore . . . .*Illinois*

Fonda Clore . . . .*Eldorado, Illinois*

Jessica Mitchell . . . .*Harrisburg, Illinois*

Kevin Clore . . . .*Harrisburg, Illinois*

DAVEY'S CUSTOMERS COME FROM ALL OVER THE WORLD!!!

Donald Johnson ....Chicago, Illinois

Danny Rutland (Mississippi College) ....Clinton, Mississippi

Jim Wilson ....Lauderdale, Mississippi

Doo Quick (Mississippi College) ....Clinton, Mississippi

Richard M. Quinn (Mississippi College) ......Clinton, Mississippi

Chris Fontan ....Florence, Mississippi

Leandro Ribeiro ....Rio de Janeiro, Brasil

Eta F. Ermlin ....Brasil

Cory DeBruhl ....Cullman, Alabama

Sandi Holder Wright "Loved It! God Bless!" ...Haleyville, Alabama

Leah Rasbury ....Haleyville, Alabama

Brenda Rasbury ....Haleyville, Alabama

Jeff Vance ....Newton, Mississippi

Bess Briggs ....Meridian, Mississippi

Judy Harwell ....Collinsville, Mississippi

Belva Osborn ....Toomsuba, Mississippi

Frances Houston ....Meridian, Mississippi

Alice Wane ....Collinsville, Mississippi

Marjorie Lockey ....Collinsville, Mississippi

Tyler Pigott ....Pearl, Mississippi

Randall Creck ....Forest, Mississippi

Tom Duffield ....Mt. Zion, Illinois

Steve Davis ....Bethany, Illinois

Brenda Key ....Oak Grove, Louisiana

Oree Cornell ....Soso, Mississippi

Jeff Madden ....Noblesville, Indiana

Amy D. Livingston ....Indianapolia, Indiana

E. Wyatt ....Laurel, Mississippi

Norma Jean Lowe "Best Food Anywhere" ......Union, Mississippi

Suzi McDill ....Decatur, Mississippi

Marcia Taylor ....Raleigh, Mississippi

Kevin Winstead ....Puckett, Mississippi

John Havard ....Little Rock, Mississippi

Bobby Joe & Gail Phipps ....Taylorsville, Mississippi

Christie Moss ....Laurel, Mississippi

DAVEY'S CUSTOMERS COME FROM ALL OVER THE WORLD!!!

DAVEY'S CUSTOMERS COME FROM ALL

Brooke Moss . . . .*Laurel, Mississippi*

Sue Cox . . . .*Humboldt, Tennessee*

Penelope Moore . . . .*Utah*

David Moore . . . .*Salt Lake City, Utah*

Eddie E. Williams, Jr. . . . .*Salt Lake City, Utah*

Tommy Baylis . . . .*Petal, Mississippi*

Carl & Linda King . . . .*Hurley, Mississippi*

Clarice & Charles Eubanks . . . .*Laurel, Mississippi*

Carrol Shepherd . . . .*Pasadena, Texas*

Allison Thames . . . .*Houston, Texas*

Baline Burgess . . . .*Natchez, Mississippi*

Josh Webb . . . .*Quitman, Mississippi*

Monroe Lofton . . . .*Brookhaven, Mississippi*

Bill Clark . . . .*Brandon, Mississippi*

Joe Normand . . . .*Bay Springs, Mississippi*

Lucretia Williams . . . .*Lena, Mississippi*

Brett Stevens . . . .*College Station, Texas*

Vickie, Jeff, Sid Stevens . . . .*College Station, Texas*

Daniel, Erica & Emmaline Listi . . . .*Louin, Mississippi*

Joe Dollar . . . .*Union, Mississippi*

Sara D. Tharpe . . . .*Union, Mississippi*

John Strickland . . . .*San Diego, California*

Bev & Emril Knott . . . .*Uncertain, Texas*

Alton Mozingo . . . .*Ellisville, Mississippi*

Nancy Beth Williams . . . .*Seminary, Mississippi*

James McIntosh . . . .*Pineville, Mississippi*

Ron Bailey . . . .*Newsoms, Virginia*

Marsha Riley . . . .*Houston, Texas*

Kathy, Fred, Lally . . . .*West Fork, Arkansas*

Tony Hardwick . . . .*Corinth, Mississippi*

Ken Dixon . . . .*Castroville, California*

Raymond Gomes . . . .*Lakeport, California*

Janice Homes . . . .*Prunedale, California*

Gladys Cherone . . . .*Copiah County*

Laureen Lockhart . . . .*Mendenhall, Mississippi*

DAVEY'S CUSTOMERS COME FROM ALL OVER THE WORLD!!!

Carmen Jefcoat ....Brandon, Mississippi
Vicki Gamann ....Carthage, Mississippi
Ella Tangle ....Carthage, Mississippi
Eugenia Smith Ferguson ....Hinds County
Barbara Rendalls ....Utica, Mississippi
Lisa Grayson ....Brandon, Mississippi
Shannon J. Adams.....................Morton, Mississippi
Mary A. Rusche ....Yazoo City, Mississippi
Trish Gregg ....Covington/Smith County
Tiffany Burch ....Smith County
Joule Fusell ....Hinds County
Gail Keele ....Ellisville
Stuart Keele ....Ellisville
Rita Ellzey ....Pascagoula, Mississippi
Kathy Robison ....Memphis, Tennessee
Jo Carol Robison ....Hoboken, New Jersey
Joe & Alice Robison....................Laurel, Mississippi
April Masengill.....................Meridian, Mississippi
Andrew Jones ....Stringer, Mississippi
Corley Jones (pastor) ....Stringer, Mississippi
Sandy Jones ....Jacksonville, Texas
Cindy Jones........................Stringer, Mississippi
Kala Hudson ....Magnolia, Arkansas
Cela Jones ....Stringer, Mississippi
Cody Oswatt ....Jackson, Mississippi
Shae Gleg ....Utica, Mississippi
Rosemary Thomas ....Natchez, Mississippi
Ron Steewart ....Madison, Mississippi
Mark Bridges ....Raymond, Mississippi
Ken McMillan ....Louisville, Mississippi
Pie Landrum ....Ovett, Mississippi
Addison Sanford......................Ovett, Mississippi
Glenda Dobbels ....Natchez, Mississippi
Angelina Smith ....Ovett, Mississippi
Dale Owens ....Atlanta, Georgia

DAVEY'S CUSTOMERS COME FROM ALL OVER THE WORLD!!!

Scott Alavaty . . . . Topeka, Kansas

Joe Flick . . . . Laurel, Mississippi

Julie Waul . . . . Columbus, Mississippi

Phil Torres . . . . Rancho Cordova, California

Troy Danes . . . . Larose, Louisiana

Maxine Busby . . . . New Augusta, Mississippi

Trey Hammock . . . . Puckett, Mississippi

Theresa Hartfield . . . . Hattiesburg, Mississippi

Bill Koch . . . . Meridian, Mississippi

Ryan Waltman . . . . Pass Christian, Mississippi

Bobby E. Cole . . . . Jackson

Deborah Elaine Cole Wharton . . . . Garden City, Kansas

Bobby & Linda Cole . . . . Bay Springs

Ralph Morgan . . . . Lauderdale, Mississippi

Vic Murphy . . . . Brandon, Mississippi

Tammy Rosson . . . . Rio Rancho, New Mexico

Matthew Rosson . . . . Rio Rancho, New Mexico

Jennifer, Lorna & Isaac Allen . . . . Rio Rancho, New Mexico

E. Tyler Sprint . . . . Carrie, Mississippi

Jim & Wanda Jenneskens . . . . Largo, Florida

Charles & Imogene Thompson . . . . Newton, Mississippi

Dan Pruitt . . . . Columbia, South Carolina

Dave McDonald . . . . Southlake, Texas

Bethany Gilbert . . . . Laurel, Mississippi

Jason Scott . . . . Meridian, Mississippi

Dwight D. Coleman, M.D. . . . . Shaker Heights, Ohio

Richard Coleman, Sr. . . . . Newton, Mississippi

Justin Young . . . . Stringer, Mississippi

Carmen Branoh . . . . Massau, Germany

D. Harris . . . . Stringer, Mississippi

Dean Bufkin . . . . Stringer, Mississippi

Molly Pitts . . . . Buckatunna, Mississippi

Sue Brown . . . . Waynesboro, Mississippi

Karen Fleming . . . . Newton, Mississippi

Mark M. Wyatt . . . . Newton, Mississippi

DAVEY'S CUSTOMERS COME FROM ALL OVER THE WORLD!!!

Mark Newcomb . . . . .Charmetti, Louisiana

Brooke Griffith . . . . .Hickory, Mississippi

Johnnie Earnest . . . . .Newton, Mississippi

John R. Clayton . . . . .Newton, Mississippi

Staci Stringer . . . . .Bloomington, Minnesota

April A. DelGiglieo . . . . .Italy

Sergin Cuterea . . . . .Sicilia, Italy

Rebecca Kyzar . . . . .Meridian, Mississippi

Ann Garvin . . . . .Newton, Mississippi

Drake Tucker . . . . : . . . . .Fort Worth, Texas

Cindy Shinfessel Anderson . . . . .Franklin, Tennessee

Jonathan Hargrave .Harrisonville, Missouri

Don George . . . . .Harrisonville, Missouri

Devon Eby . . . . .Resaca, Georgia

Jerry Eby . . . . .Resaca, Georgia

C. Michael Bullet . . . . .Louin/Madison, Mississippi

Jim Murphy .Little Rock (Chicago)

Jane Harthcock . . . . .Woodstock, Georgia

Delia and Tommy Harthcock . . . .

Harvey Ed Keen . . . .

Bo Burrough . . . .

Herman "Thunderfoot" Wear . . . . .Chattanooga, Tennessee

Lynjorae Williams .Carthage, Mississippi

Linda Williams . . . . .Carthage, Mississippi

Ruth Williams . . . . .Carthage, Mississippi

Tom Kendall . . . . .Austin, Texas

Chad Barney . . . . .Biloxi, Mississippi

Eva Foster . . . . .Haleyville, Alabama

Dorris J. Diehl . . . . .Haleyville, Alabama

Patrick Lewis . . . . .Meridian, Mississippi

Shane Hegwood . . . . .Meridian, Mississippi

Mike Bennett . . . . .Columbia, Mississippi

Bobby Strock . . . . .Laurel, Mississippi

Kevin Jones . . . . .Laurel, Mississippi

Rev. Eddie Lee Jones . . . . .Starkville, Mississippi

DAVEY'S CUSTOMERS COME FROM ALL OVER THE WORLD!!!

Ken Henderson . . . . .Wilmer, Alabama
Timm Forbes . . . . .Louisville, Kentucky
Jack Carver . . . . .Louisville, Kentucky
Brad S. Hammons . . . . .Pineville, Mississippi
Frankie Hammons . . . . .Pineville, Mississippi
Ron Neal . . . . .Southaven, Mississippi
Jimmy Parker . . . . .Stringer, Mississippi
Mrs. Merry Bender-Jones . . . . .Starkville, Mississippi
Mary Williams . . . . .Louin, Mississippi
George E. Smith . . . . .Laurel, Mississippi
Michael Bilberry . . . . .Houston, Texas
David Caulfield . . . . .Hattiesburg, Mississippi
Sandra Dudley .Hattiesburg, Mississippi
Teresa McRaney . . . . .Bassfield, Mississippi
Martha Abercrombie . . . . .Collins, Mississippi
Nancy Garvin .Beaumont, Mississippi
Ginger Burks .Hattiesburg, Mississippi
Sherry Burnham .Seminary, Mississippi
Kathy Burch . . . . .Richton, Mississippi
Gina Cleaver . . . . .Petal, Mississippi
Judy Cassell . . . . .Petal, Mississippi
Connie Trotter .Hattiesburg, Mississippi
Marilyn Keene .Hattiesburg, Mississippi
Dianne McKee . . . . .Gautier, Mississippi
Jayce Brown . . . . .Heidelberg, Mississippi
Winnie Smith . . . . .Heidelberg, Mississippi
Lillian Welborn .Heidelberg, Mississippi
Robert & Pam Lind . . . . .Kiln, Mississippi
Rudolph & Gail Ellis . . . . .Newton, Mississippi
Ron Herrington . . . . .St. Petersburg, Florida
Bo Dexton . . . . .Meridian, Mississippi
Dr. David & Katie Sullivan . . . . .Laurel, Mississippi
Elizabeth & Ann Marie Sullivan . . . . .Laurel, Mississippi
Rickie Fleming . . . .
Bessie Wray . . . . .Colorado Springs, Colorado

DAVEY'S CUSTOMERS COME FROM ALL OVER THE WORLD!!!

Mary A. Jackson Jennings ....*Laurel, Mississippi*
Linda Walsh ....*Milwaukee, Wisconsin*
Judy Johns ....*Colorado Springs, Colorado*
Andrew Johns...................*Colorado Springs, Colorado*
Shamira Smith.................*Colorado Springs, Colorado*
Danny Weston ....*Milwaukee, Wisconsin*
Pierea Weston ....*Milwaukee, Wisconsin*
De'Ja Davenport ....*Milwaukee, Wisconsin*
Dale Harrison ....*Colorado Springs, Colorado*
Shalicia Walsh ....*Atlanta, Georgia*
Angela Crenshaw ....*Meridian, Mississippi*
Dr. Scott Crenshaw .....*Mt Zion Baptist Church/ Meridian, MS*
Kenneth Lewis ....*Laurel, Mississippi*
Tommy & Rita Davis ....*Meridian, Mississippi*
Reggie Litt........................*Braselton, Georgia*
Bob Saxton ....*Laurel, Mississippi*
Guitarist with Patsy Cline - Carl Perkins, Billy Walker, Martha
Carson, Charlie Louvin, Gene Vincent, & Others
Janie Hodge ....*Bay Springs, Mississippi*
Joan Deese........................*Gold Hill, Oregon*
Helen Massey ....*Bay Springs, Mississippi*
Cynthia Gomez ....*Eugene, Oregon*
Janice Brady ....*Louin, Mississippi*
Ruth Edmandson-Johnson ....*Sutter Creek, California*
Brittni Hollingshead ....*Laurel, Mississippi*
Brook Hollinsghead ....*Laurel, Mississippi*
Eric Hollingshead ....*Laurel, Mississippi*
Debra & Johnny Chatham ....*Lena, Mississippi*
Don & Ann Thornton ....
Bobby & Phyllis Holder.................*Laurel, Mississippi*
Renault Herrington ....*Senioa, Georgia*
Mel & Beth Hollidge ....*Concord, New Hampshire*
Brenda McPhail ....*Colllins, Mississippi*
Glenn & Peggy Shoemake ....*Boggie, Mississippi*
Gregory Rustin ....

223

DAVEY'S CUSTOMERS COME FROM ALL OVER THE WORLD!!!

Jeannie Rustin . . . .*Laurel, Mississippi*

Ernest Gray . . . .*Petal, Mississippi*

Albealious Watts . . . .*Sumrall, Mississippi*

David Swysgood . . . .*Siloam Springs, Arkansas*

Cecil J. Ashford . . . .*Laurel, Mississippi*

Haile T. Gaddy . . . .*Laurel, Mississippi*

Audy Smith . . . .*Corona, California*

Rene Galarza . . . .*Vale, North Carolina*

Steve Price . . . .*Ozark, Alabama*

Anthony Sorey . . . .*Pineville, Mississippi*

Brant & Gayle Cochran . . . .*Brroklyn, Mississippi*

James Blackburn . . . .*Ozark, Alabama*

Ronnie Carter . . . .*Fortworth, Texas*

Randy McWharter . . . .*Laurel, Mississippi*

Wanda Payton . . . .*Bay Springs, Mississippi*

Glady Kelly . . . .*Bay Springs, Mississippi*

Donna Parker . . . .*Stringer, Mississippi*

Opal Warren . . . .*Bay Springs, Mississippi*

Nila Cromwell . . . .*Bay Springs, Mississippi*

Alice Windham . . . .*Bay Springs, Mississippi*

Shelita Burns . . . .*Jackson, Mississippi*

Sherry G. Breland . . . .*Stringer, Mississippi*

Becky G. Rayner . . . .*Stringer, Mississippi*

Bradley "M" Peak . . . .*Tuscaloosa, Alabama*

Ed Cooper . . . .*Tuscaloosa, Alabama*

Michael Shane Cooper . . . .*Gulfport, Mississippi*

Jim R. Hoda . . . .*Kiln, Mississippi*

Kurt Feadus . . . .*Huntsville, Alabama*

Billy Johnson . . . .*Hickory, Mississippi*

Adam T. Robinke . . . .*Rochester, New York*

Dorothy Little . . . .*Meridian, Mississippi*

Sheila King . . . .*Taylorsville, Mississippi*

Fernando L. Billings . . . .*Mobile, Alabama*

Rev. Malachi Jones . . . .*Prichard, Alabama*

Phillip Warren . . . .*Brandon, Mississippi*

DAVEY'S CUSTOMERS COME FROM ALL OVER THE WORLD!!!

Melanie Warren . . . . .Brandon, Mississippi

Lee V. Marshall . . . . .Flint, Michigan

Eddie Stapleton . . . . .Raleigh, Mississippi

Douglas Smiley . . . . .Newton, Mississippi

Brian Brashear . . . . .Seymour, Missouri

Andy Roedel . . . . .Frannie, Wyoming

Jane Galasso . . . . .Grey Bull, Wyoming

Ken Henderson . . . . .Wilmer, Alabama

Bobb Jackson . . . . .Dacula, Georgia

Lacey Bergman . . . . .Augusta, Wisconsin

Albert Daniels . . . . .Kiln, Mississippi

Kelly Compton . . . . .Ashland, Wisconson

Louis Sumers . . . . .Kiln, Mississippi

Darren Ladner . . . . .Kiln, Mississippi

Chris Hoda . . . . .Kiln, Mississippi

James McDaniel . . . . .Kiln, Mississippi

Randy Daniels . . . . .Kiln, Mississippi

Wayne Pliett . . . . .Brandon, Mississippi

Dave Reed . . . . .Fair Haven, Vermont

Ferhand Delisle . . . . .St. Petersburg, Florida

Lisa Lindstrom . . . . .Southbridge, Maine

Glory Lapierre . . . . .Southbridge, Maine

Hemi Avenett . . . . .Rose Hill, Mississippi

Jay Murphy . . . . .Chunky, Mississippi

John Peconom . . . . .Washington, DC

Doug Mooneyhan .Woodstock, Georgia

Brent Dixon . . . . .Anacortes, Washington

Dennis Woods . . . . .Houston, Texas

Jerry Wayne Hilbun .Houston, Texas

Stephen Newcomb . . . . .Farmerville, Louisiana

Jack Jarrell . . . . .Laurel, Mississippi

Kala Peebles .Minneapolis, Minnesota

Warren Estes .Bay Springs, Mississippi

Sheryl Peebles . . . . .Newton, Mississipi

Robbie Hinton . . . . .Soso, Mississippi

DAVEY'S CUSTOMERS COME FROM ALL OVER THE WORLD!!!

Brent Quick .... Waynesboro, Mississippi
Staci Maddox .... Ridgeland, Mississippi
Dianna Conner .... Waynesboro, Mississippi
Charmaine McGowan .... Jackson, Mississippi
Michael Wynne .... Chattanooga, Tennessee
Jason Dedwylder .... Quitman, Mississippi
Sherry Chancellor .... Ellisville, Mississippi
Marlo Dorsey .... Ellisville, Mississippi
Mike Crabtree .... Stonewall, Mississippi
Kelly Jones .... Mize, Mississippi
Ted A. Roland .... Picayune, Mississippi
Russell Drury .... Carriere, Mississippi
Amy Wilberding .... Hattiesburg, Mississippi
Randy Adams .... Laurel, Mississippi
Donna Adams .... Laurel, Mississippi
Sumer Adams .... Laurel, Mississippi
Ricky Adams .... Laurel, Mississippi
Delone Adams .... Laurel, Mississippi
Richie Salem .... Birmingham, Alabama
Ron Barham .... Madison, Mississippi
Rex Johnson .... Boca Raton, Florida
Claire Lynch .... Hollywood, California
Michael Lynch .... Hollywood, California
Chad Davis .... Locust Grove, Georgia
Chris Wall .... Brandon, Mississippi
Wendell Walker & family .... Pendleton, South Carolina
Jordan Walker .... Decatur, Mississippi
Steve Scites .... Collinsville, Mississippi
Dr. Ryan Logan .... Jackson, Mississippi
Son Lam, MD .... Corinth, Mississippi
Kenny & Renee Jones .... Gatlinburg, Tennessee
Chris & Toi Fausak .... Mobile, Alabama
Stan & Virginia Riles .... Laurel, Mississippi
Dale Donaghy & Jasselin .... Barton, Vermont
Mellissa Makin .... Bay City, Michigan

DAVEY'S CUSTOMERS COME FROM ALL OVER THE WORLD!!!

Carmen Simmons . . . .

Martha Swearington . . . .

Shirley Lee . . . .

Keith Hancock . . . . .Sandersville, Mississippi

Brent Blackwell . . . . .Laurel, Mississippi

T. Q. Sims . . . .

Dwight Jackson . . . . .Preston, Mississippi

Dawn B. Smith . . . . .Scooba, Mississippi

David Misars . . . . .Madison, Mississippi

Eddie Middleton . . . . .Vossburg, Mississippi

Scott Wilson .Hattiesburg, Mississippi

Shannon Daughdrill . . . . .Petal, Mississippi

Ronnie Russell . . . . .Lumberton, Mississippi

Jim Daughdrill . . . . .Purvis, Mississippi

Pastor Harold Laird . . . . .Lake, Mississippi

Steve Ehman . . . . .Tipton, Indiana

Kevin Woods . . . . .Laurel, Mississippi

Michel Poirier . . . . .Quebec, Canada

Michael Barton . . . . .Quebec, Canada

Oliver Quite . . . . .Quebec, Canada

April Taylor . . . . .Stringer, Mississippi

Wayne & Carolyn Hall . . . . .Forest, Mississippi

John A. Welborn . . . . .Kiln, Mississippi

Nicky Ferguson . . . . .Kiln, Mississippi

Nathan Stricklen . . . . .Sequin, Texas

John Woodard . . . . .Columbus, Mississippi

Mark Ward . . . . .Columbus, Mississippi

Tom Buckley . . . . .Columbus, Mississippi

Louisa Roussell .Columbus, Mississippi

A. J. Budging . . . . .Columbus, Mississippi

Mark Vibe . . . . .Columbus, Mississippi

Eli Sandelhaus . . . . .St. Louis, Missouri

David Parnell . . . . .Pell City, Alabama

Robert L. Brown . . . . .Laurel, Mississippi

Jennifer Griffeth . . . . .Seminary, Mississippi

DAVEY'S CUSTOMERS COME FROM ALL OVER THE WORLD!!!

Pam Brumlee . . . . *Ovett, Mississippi*

Paul B. Johnson . . . . *Seminary, Mississippi*

Regina Gutchens . . . . *Ellisville, Mississippi*

Lela Bryan . . . . *Bay Springs, Mississippi*

Jo Calhoun . . . . *Wilmer, Arkansas*

Christine Rowl . . . . *Lyles, Tennessee*

Meranda Greene . . . . *Heber Springs, Arkansas*

Richard Phelps . . . . *Kewanee, Illinois*

Robert Hemphill . . . . *Sauk Rapids, Minnesota*

Cheryl L. Hemphill . . . . *Sauk Rapids, Minnesota*

Benji Shoe . . . . *Walnut Ridge, Arkansas*

Kenneth R. Dye . . . . *Bastrup, Louisiana*

Betty Chesnut . . . . *Russellville, Alabama*

Jimmy & Mary Swain . . . . *Raleigh, Mississippi*

Carl Cobb . . . . *Savannah, Georgia*

Michael Bruneau . . . . *Peace River, Alberta, Canada*

Sonya Frank . . . . *Gulfport, Mississippi*

Gordon Espelien . . . . *Spring Grove, Minnesota*

David Wright . . . . *Rye, Arkansas*

Randall Creel . . . . *Forest, Mississippi*

Jerry Holmes . . . . *Morton, Mississippi*

Kenny Long . . . . *Lake, Mississippi*

Frank Morgan . . . . *Forest, Mississippi*

Matt Jernigan . . . . *Murfreesboro, Tennessee*

Chris Jernigan . . . . *Murfreesboro, Tennessee*

Nicole & Brittany Jernigan . . . . *Murfreesboro, Tennessee*

Chris Barton . . . . *Birmingham, Alabama*

Pamela Summerville . . . . *Laurel, Mississippi*

Jessica Huffman . . . . *Starkville, Mississippi*

John Ferguson . . . . *Niota, Illinois*

Nancy Ferguson . . . . *Niota, Illinois*

Jill McEnaney . . . . *Columbus, Ohio*

Buzz & Joy McEnaney . . . . *Springfield, Ohio*

Lynn Lindsey . . . . *Seattle, Washington*

Lex Lindsey . . . . *Seattle, Washington*

DAVEY'S CUSTOMERS COME FROM ALL
OVER THE WORLD!!!

Ned Turnball . . . .*Laurel, Mississippi*

Bill & Betty Carpenter . . . .*Houston, Texas*

Danny Thompson . . . .*Runnelstown, Mississippi*

Chris Madrid . . . .*McKinney, Texas*

Jasper Wall . . . .*Bastrop, Louisiana*

Billy G. Rayner . . . .*Jasper County Circuit Clerk*

KeJuan Lee . . . .

Vickie Downs . . . .*Statesville, North Carolina*

Michael Daryn . . . .*Statesville, North Carolina*

Bennett T. Smith . . . .*Bossier City, Louisiana*

Joleen Moore . . . .*Meridian, Mississippi*

Kelly Nelson . . . .*Raleigh, Mississippi*

Rev. & Mrs. Gerald Chaney . . . .*Chunky, Mississippi*

Tony Soldinie . . . .*Petal, Mississippi* ·

Randy Burge . . . .*Poplarville, Mississippi*

Kay Burnage . . . .*Meridian, Mississippi*

Mattie Fern Stevens Pinkham . . . .*Newton, Mississippi*

Iva Pauline Turbville . . . .*Kemper County*

Dorothy Shirley . . . .*Meridian, Mississippi*

Matthew Grayson . . . .*Collinsville, Mississippi*

Ed & Jean Jordon . . . .*Seminary, Mississippi*

George & Donna Joe Pettinger . . . .*Michigan*

Chad Cook . . . .*Houston, Texas*

Anna Keller . . . .*Knoxville, Tennessee*

Opal Keller . . . .*Meridian, Mississippi*

Bob Keller . . . .*Meridian, Mississippi*

Jenny Wright . . . .*Rison, Arizona*

William H. Downs . . . .*Rural Retreat, Virginia*

Frances M. Downs . . . .*Rural Retreat, Virginia*

Chris Brakebush . . . .*Westfield, Wisconsin*

Megan Brakebush . . . .*Westfield, Wisconsin*

Brenda Thornton . . . .*Gilmer, Texas*

Sue Savell . . . .*Union, Mississippi*

Lynda Farron . . . .*Hickory, Mississippi*

Nathan Brooks . . . .*Ovett, Mississippi*

DAVEY'S CUSTOMERS COME FROM ALL OVER THE WORLD!!!

Wesley Bender . . . . .Laurel, Mississippi
Laura Jones . . . . .Merced, California
Patricia Boyles . . . . .Waynesboro, Mississippi
Mary Shedd . . . . .Laurel, Mississippi
Junior Shedd . . . . .Laurel, Mississippi
Kamron Gooch . . . . .Laurel, Mississippi
Jessica Williams .Buckatunna, Mississippi
Debbie Gooch . . . . .Laurel, Mississippi
Vernice Hopkins . . . .
Etheline Perry .Waynesboro, Mississippi
Flora Shedd . . . . .Eucutta, Mississippi
Effie Lee Shedd . . . . .Laurel, Mississippi
Kathy Ritchey . . . . .Laurel, Mississippi
John Brown . . . . .Waynesboro, Mississippi
John Seeper . . . . .Waynesboro, Mississippi
Margaret Strickland . . . . .Ellisville, Mississippi
Beverly W. Boone . . . . .Moselle, Mississippi
Pastor Harley Williams . . . . .Girard, Oklahoma
Ray Doggett . . . . .Laurel, Mississippi
Don Houston Wood .Laurel, Mississippi
Evelyn Williamson . . . . .Soso, Mississippi
Scotty Russell . . . . .Decatur, Mississippi
Harold & Martha Ann Nelson . . . . .Pineville, Mississippi
Tom Box . . . . .Clinton, Mississippi
Katie Morgan . . . . .Alexandria, Virginia
Chris Morgan . . . . .Alexandria, Virginia
Margie Mae Morgan Pugh . . . . .Newton, Mississippi
M'liss Ann Pang . . . . .Kaneohe, Hawaii
Tracy Burmeiste .Bloomington, Minnesota
Billy & Delores Wigington . . . . .Laurel, Mississippi
Darren & Jamie Patterson . . . . .West Monroe, Louisiana
Dean Duncan . . . . .Valparaiso, Indiana
Dave Barkholaer . . . . .Chambersburl, Pennsylvania
James Landis . . . . .Jonestown, Pennsylvania
Leroy J. Strite . . . . Bay Springs, Mississippi

DAVEY'S CUSTOMERS COME FROM ALL OVER THE WORLD!!!

Jim Zadzow . . . . .Eagle, Idaho
Rita Gunn . . . . .Mobile, Alabama
Ruth Gunn . . . . .Bay Springs, Mississippi
Libby Middleton . . . . .Bellefontaine, Mississippi
Greg Anderson .Farmerville, Louisiana
Shelia Luker . . . . .Richton, Mississippi
Katlyn Luker . . . . .Richton, Mississippi
Alice Yelverton . . . . .Laurel, Mississippi
Judy Sellers . . . . .Laurel, Mississippi
Brandon Westbrook . . . . .Memphis, Tennessee
Thomas E. Brown . . . . .Bay Springs, Mississippi
Billy Joe Low . . . . .Selma, California
Brandt Nichols . . . . .Laurel, Mississippi
Sandi Sevier . . . . .Meridian, Mississippi
Jayce Band . . . . .Meridian, Mississippi
Lena Linton . . . . .Meridian, Mississippi
Chi Phillips . . . . .Houston, Texas
Aaron Davis . . . . .Houston, Texas
Dr. Benjamin J. Hodges . . . .
Paul A. Little, D.C. . . . .
Dr. John B. Harrison . . . .
Joyce Luke . . . . .Hickory, Mississippi
Janet Dunavant .Newton, Mississippi
Kevin Bentley . . . . .Rose Hill, Mississippi
E. W. Goodwin .Vossburg, Mississippi
Bo Clark . . . . .Newton, Mississippi
Kelli Young. . . . . .Port Charlotte, Florida
Jay Stanle . . . . .Port Charlotte, Florida
Chuck Norris. . . . . .Louin, Mississippi
Cindy Doolittle . . . . .Bay Springs, Mississippi
Shelby Doolittle . . . .
Savannah Doolittle . . . . .Bay Springs, Mississippi
Ted Horn . . . .(Estes Barbershop)
Ronald Dare . . . . .Vidalia, Louisiana
Thomas Waren .River Ridge, Louisiana

DAVEY'S CUSTOMERS COME FROM ALL OVER THE WORLD!!!

Frank and Judy Leatherwood . . . . *Terry, Mississippi*

Marilyn Gary . . . . *California*

Patsy Gary . . . . *Newton, Mississippi*

Sonya Johnson . . . . *Laurel, Mississippi*

Charity Wilson . . . . *Waynesboro, Mississippi*

Pat Steiner . . . . *Laurel, Mississippi*

Roger, Carla & Myleia Shirley . . . . *Chunky, Mississippi*

Kendall Blake . . . . *Laurel, Mississippi*

Robert & Bonnie McLaurin . . . . *Laurel, Mississippi*

Keith Winfield . . . . *Starkville, Mississippi*

B. Ellis . . . . *Newton, Mississippi*

Lynda Ellis . . . . *Heidelberg, Mississippi*

Gloria Saitta . . . . *Apopka, Florida*

Rev. Allen Shortridge . . . . *Meridian, Mississippi*

Marins Van Der Merwe . . . . *South Africa*

Laura Singley . . . . *Hattiesburg, Mississippi*

Carrie Bauer . . . . *Stringer, Mississippi*

Lillous Faye Shoemaker (wonderful!) . . . . *Bay Springs*

Curtis B. Alexander (very good!) . . . . *Bay Springs*

James Laird . . . . *Laurel, Mississipi*

Charles Murphrey . . . . *Birmingham, Alabama*

Heather Milner . . . . *Taylorsville, Mississippi*

Kelly Astin . . . . *Laurel, Mississippi*

James B. Eiben Jr. *Ridgeland, Mississippi*

Tracy & Vicki Tucker . . . . *Meridian, Mississippi*

Tom & Susan Frazier . . . . *Meridian, Mississippi*

Rudy Vance . . . . *Carthage, Mississippi*

Shirley Vance . . . . *Gary, Texas*

Delores Canuby . . . . *Panama City Beach, Florida*

Margaret Vance . . . . *Scardaci, Cario, New York*

Ben Bacter . . . . *Newcastle upon Tyne, England*

Brandi Easterling . . . . *Waynesboro, Mississippi*

Michael & Anne LaBelle . . . . *Wylie, Texas*

Walter E. Gray, Jr. . . . . *Carthage, Mississippi*

Lonnie Ray Littleton . . . . *Downsville, Louisiana*

DAVEY'S CUSTOMERS COME FROM ALL OVER THE WORLD!!!

Marcus Sparks (Awesome!) . . . . .Memphis, Tennessee

Bettye W. Dobbs (Great!) . . . . .Decatur, Mississippi

Verna M. Rosh (G-O-O-D!) . . . . .Decatur, Mississippi

---

"Flyin Bryan" Huke from ROCK 104 . . . . .Laurel, Mississippi

Andy Webb ROCK 104 . . . . .Laurel, Mississippi

Tom Colt- ROCK 104 Morning Crew . . . . .Laurel, Mississippi

Davey, these are the people who ate at Davey's Restaurant
June 18, 2008
Radio Station Rock 104 in Laurel, MS

Lorrey Collins . . . . .Stringer, Mississiippi

Sharron Smith . . . . .Stringer, Mississippi

Gus & Ruby Vallas .Decatur, Mississippi

Susan Marshall . . . . .Tennessee

Tala Stand Grooe . . . . .Fair Haven, New York

Amy & Carl Crawford . . . . .Kingsport, Tennessee

Gail & Dalton Thibodeaux . . . . .Magee, Mississippi

Terry L. Wooley .LaMirada, California

Rita Taylor . . . . .Laurel, Mississippi

Ray Taylor . . . . .Laurel, Mississippi

David & Ellen Taylor . . . . .Laurel, Mississippi

Randy Judge . . . . .Lake, Mississippi

Brook Maughon . . . . .Atlanta, Georgia

Lynn Johnson .Birmingham, Alabama

Shawanda Moore . . . . .Birmingham, Alabama

Rita Jones . . . . .Birmingham, Alabama

Sheila Clingman .Holly Pond, Alabama

Sheri Peason . . . . .Meridian, Mississippi

Kevin Gressett . . . . .Chunky, Mississippi

Msgt. Billie Johnson "Catfish" . . . . .Cullman, Alabama

Jeff Dorsey . . . . .Jackson, Mississippi

Jerry Todd . . . . .Ridgeland, Mississippi

David & Chelsy Walters . . . . .Ellisville, Mississippi

DAVEY'S CUSTOMERS COME FROM ALL OVER THE WORLD!!!

David H. Walters . . . . .Moselle, Mississippi

Wayne & Rose Wicker . . . . .Homewood, Mississippi

Hilton & Elouise Winstead . . . . .Pelahatchie, Mississippi

Frannie Lewis . . . . .Philadelphia, Mississippi

Toy & Jared McLaurin . . . . .Bay Springs

Josh & Alison Garner . . . . .Limestone, Tennessee

Chris Blair & Mercy Anderson . . . . .Lake, Mississippi

Donald O'Cain . . . . .Magee, Mississippi

Jeff Mueller . . . . .Spring City, Tennessee

James Henderson . . . . .Evansville, Tennessee

Cheryl Comans . . . . .Decatur, Mississippi

Elone Rogers . . . . .Bay Springs, Mississippi

Vickey Bingham .Bay Springs, Mississippi

Keith Winfield . . . . .Starkville, Mississippi

Bonnie Lindsey . . . . .Riverside, California

David Burt . . . . .Newton, Mississippi

Janie Mitts Moore . . . . .Houston, Texas

Castlen Moore . . . . .Houston, Texas

Dee Moore . . . . .Houston, Texas

Cory Kennedy . . . . .Reno, Nevada

Billy Mitts III . . . . .Meridian, Mississippi

Kayla Blackwell . . . . .Soso, Mississippi

Jerry, Martha, Summer Gable . . . . .Raleigh, Mississippi

Sheila Frazier . . . . .Taylorsville, Mississippi

Ted, Shelby, & Brandon . . . .

Herbert Thibodeaux . . . . .Jackson, Mississippi

Emanuella Grinberg . . . . .New York, New York

Cecelia Koltura .YorbaUnda, California

Roger Noyes .Mountain View, California

Butch Culimn . . . . .Laurel, Mississippi

Randy Whitehead . . . . .Baxter, Tennessee

Brent Whitehead . . . . .Baxter, Tennessee

Adriene Slaymaker . . . . .Anchorage, Arkansas

Trent King . . . . .Baxter, Tennessee

Tannee Whitehead . . . . .Anchorage, Arkansas

Brett Gardner . . . . .Garden City, Kansas

DAVEY'S CUSTOMERS COME FROM ALL OVER THE WORLD!!!

Todd Oliver & Shirley Brown ....

Lou Boyles .... Palm Desert, California

Wesley Hall .... Taylorsville, Mississippi

Guadaloupe Sambrano .... Garland, Utah

Eduvina Garcia .... Tremanton, Utah

Lilia Lopez .... West Haven, Utah

Laura Contreras....................... Michoacan, Mexico

Jocelynn Alanis .... Knoxville, Tennessee

Sabrina Thames ....

Mira Patrick .... Newton, Mississippi

Carman Williams .... Neosho, Missouri

Essie Bingham........................ Newton, Mississippi

Beverly Aerbuson .... Newton, Mississippi

Evone Pruitt .... Newton, Mississippi

Barbara McGehee .... Neosha, Missouri

Vickie Scroggins .... Neosha, Missouri

Marilyn Grissom .... Laurel, Mississippi

Connie Allegritti .... San Jose, California

Andrew Hveem .... San Jose, California

Jimmie Sue Bates .... Laurel, Mississippi

Jeffrey Massey .... Shreveport, Louisiana

Robb Lacey........................ Shreveport, Louisiana

Patsy and Johnny Matlock .... Union, Mississippi

Larry Muse .... Union, Mississippi

Troy Manchester .... Newton, Mississippi

Sebestine Davis Torok .... Erie, Pennsylvania

Scottie Lee Davis .... New York, New York

Celestine Davis .... Erie, Pennsylvania

Keith Hinkle .... Pinson, Alabama

Leah Chinchilla .... MSU

Anastasia Woodard .... Manhattan, Kansas

Rev. Andrew & Danielle Mills .... Senatobia, Mississippi

Shannon Sims .... Taylorsville, Mississippi

Bobby Harper .... Brandon, Mississippi

Tommy Fairley .... Petal, Mississippi

Senator Billy C. Hudson & Wife ....

DAVEY'S CUSTOMERS COME FROM ALL OVER THE WORLD!!!

Dallen Davis . . . . .Slidell, Louisiana
Jaseyn Harris . . . . .Westbank
Caleb Buckley . . . . .Westbank
Debbie Everett .Hattiesburg, Mississippi
Lois Pennington . . . . .Decatur, Mississippi
CArolyn & Eric Edison . . . .
Marty & Monica Cooley .Soso, Mississippi
Samantha Grell . . . . .Chico, California
Gale & Bill Bell . . . . .El Cerrito, California
Janet Jackson .W. Hartford, Conneticut
Heather Layton . . . . .Douglasville, Georgia
Freida Layton . . . . .Georgia
Edwin, Angie, Chandler & Conner Clark . . . . . .Lake, Mississippi
Brenda Crosby . . . . .Lake, Mississippi
Charlie Peacock . . . . .Albertville, Alabama
Scott French . . . . .Laurel, Mississippi
Michael D. Boswell .Gulfport, Mississippi
Rachel King . . . . .Gulfport, Mississippi
Debbie Stewart . . . . .Gulfport, Mississippi
Marcus D. Cuevas . . . . .Pass Christian, Mississippi
Wiliam Richardson . . . .
Steve Bugby . . . . .Forest, Mississippi
Jamie Veazey . . . . .Forest, Mississippi
Hiram Richardson . . . . .Forest, Mississippi
John Stringer . . . . .Houston, Texas
Donald Pertrit . . . . .Billings, Montana
Ray & Amanda Spence . . . . .Union, Mississippi
Bill & Glenda McKinion . . . . .Collinsville, Mississippi
Doug & Lydia Mesta .Pensacola, Florida
Bill Mathis . . . .(Johnny Stringer's Buddy)
Dorothy Combest . . . .
Robert Combest . . . . .Gautier, Mississippi
Ed Lock . . . . .Warrensburg, Illinois
Brent Damery . . . . .Blue Mound, Illinois
Frank Diem . . . . .York, Pennsylvania

DAVEY'S CUSTOMERS COME FROM ALL OVER THE WORLD!!!

Dr. & Mrs. Chris Collins . . . . Vicksburg, Mississippi

Armond, Jackie & Amanda Newton . . . .

Ed, Roseno, Tacarra, Ivy, & Verbrasia Williamson . . . .

Moriah Williamson . . . .

Dawn Moore . . . . Hamilton, Mississippi

Gene Laton . . . . Columbia, Mississippi

Mr. & Mrs. Micah Welborn . . . . Laurel, Mississippi

Greg, Rhonda & Shelby Smith . . . . Laurel, Mississippi

Ted Ratcliff . . . . Brookhaven, Mississippi

Bob Halford . . . . Forest, Mississippi

Kristin Chaney . . . . Little Rock, Mississippi

Scott Hire . . . . Decatur, Mississippi

Betty James Bradley . . . . Mize, Mississippi

Larry Looney . . . . Ellisville, Mississippi

Jim Kelly . . . .

Wes Clark . . . . Pontotoc, Mississippi

Mark & Melissa Balton . . . . Ellisville, Mississippi

Steve & Selena Swink . . . . Forest, Mississippi

Sherrie Reeves . . . . Forest, Mississippi

Greg Swink . . . . Eldon, Missouri

Frank Nichols . . . . Minneapolis, Minnesota

James McHenry . . . . San Bernadino, California

Marcia Murillo . . . . Chino, California

Danny Gregory . . . . Newton, Mississippi

Alison Hinton Odom . . . . Flora, Mississippi

Brian Barlow . . . . Madison, Mississippi

Dee Dee Richardson . . . . Meridian, Mississippi

Steve & Kimmie Jarrell . . . . Laurel, Mississippi

Hillary Lowe . . . . Brandon, Mississippi

Garrett Lowe . . . . Brandon, Mississippi

Regina Parker . . . . Stringer, Mississippi

Mike Dozier . . . . Hattiesburg, Mississippi

Kale Poore . . . . Laurel, Mississippi

Nate Nickey . . . . Flardrea, South Dakota

Berdie Steve . . . . Heidelberg, Mississippi

DAVEY'S CUSTOMERS COME FROM ALL OVER THE WORLD!!!

May McGeisey . . . . .Philadelphia, Mississippi

Frances Darley . . . . .Mize, Mississippi

Jean Windham . . . . .Bay Springs, Mississippi

Glenda Wheeler .Laurel, Mississippi

Sandra Wargue .Stringer, Mississippi

Peggy Walker . . . . .Heidelberg, Mississippi

Pat Caldwell . . . . .Laurel, Mississippi

Marie Corley . . . . .Bay Springs, Mississippi

Dorothy Moss . . . . .Laurel, Mississippi

Kathy Turman . . . . .Maryville, Tennessee

Thomas Dobbs .Laurel, Mississippi

Inch T. Gandy . . . . .Hattiesburg, Mississippi

Clay Hammock . . . . .Hattiesburg, Mississippi

Emi Hammons . . . . .Mexico

Jan & Ron Brown . . . . .Jackson, Mississippi

Rhonda Sutter . . . . .Cut Off, Louisiana

Rene Duet . . . . .Cut Off, Louisiana

Pam Pike . . . . .Cut Off, Louisiana

Art Montey . . . . .Excel, Alabama

Josh Rigdon . . . .

Penny Jones . . . . .Jackson, Mississippi

Jo Ann Hardy . . . . .Walnut Grove, Mississippi

Ruby Thomas .Philadelphia, Mississippi

Greg Simon . . . . .Pelahatchie, Mississippi

Dr. Adam Strebeck . . . . .Meridian, Mississippi

Bonnie May Coleman . . . . .Ridgeland, Mississippi

Brennen Riddle . . . . .Rome, Georgia

Jason McKinock .Jackson, Mississippi

Barbara Gilliam . . . . .Pontiac, Michigan

Martha Gant . . . . .Blythwood, South Carolina

Kenneth R. Owen . . . . .Meridian, Mississippi

James M. Vance . . . . .Meridian, Mississippi

Randy Smith . . . . .Laurel, Mississippi

Dincia Irabin .Little Rock, Arkansas

Tandy Thomas . . . . .Salina, Kansas

DAVEY'S CUSTOMERS COME FROM ALL OVER THE WORLD!!!

Mary Logan .... Enterprise, Mississippi
Beradine Denham .... Enterprise, Mississippi
Robert & Alatha Whitman .... Union, Mississippi
Kenneth Ramsey .... Spearsville, Louisiana
Lance Jefcoat .... Soso, Mississippi
Marlene Chandler .... Laurel, Mississippi
Jimmy Chandler .... Laurel, Mississippi
Leanne Chandler .... Laurel, Mississippi
Kay Smith .... Collins, Mississippi
Ellen Russell .... Sumrall, Mississippi
John & Melissa Perry ....
Helen Butler .... Raleigh, Mississippi
John L. Butler .... Raleigh, Mississippi
Herbert & Dixie Simpson .... Brandon, Mississippi
Bobbie L. Bishop .... Brandon, Mississippi
Jeff Vance .... Newton, Mississippi
Debbie Stringer .... Jackson, Mississippi
Rev. J. L. Holloway ....
Elaine Shelby .... Taylorsville, Mississippi
Billy & Joann Rowell .... Pascagoula, Mississippi
Donzie M. Spears .... Meridian, Mississippi
Bettie J. Kakes .... Newton, Mississippi
John Lawrence Butler .... Raleigh, Mississippi
Colleen Butler .... Raleigh, Mississippi
Wayne Kairdolf .... New Orleans, Louisiana
Myra Patrick .... Heidelberg, Mississippi
Zachery & Jennifer Patrick .... Heidelberg, Mississippi
Jason Enroth .... Gulfport, Mississippi
Eddie Duncan .... Saucier, Mississippi
Ellis Ray Williamson .... Saucier, Mississippi
Robert Grissom .... Saucier, Mississippi
Sheree Zbylot .... Jackson, Mississippi
Margaret Carter Lora .... Mobile, Alabama
Ms. Catherine Carter Clark .... Milwaukee, Wisconsin
Katrina Manes .... Diana, Texas

DAVEY'S CUSTOMERS COME FROM ALL OVER THE WORLD!!!

Kenneth Alexander . . . . .Umatilla, Florida

Dannette Lanier . . . . .Little Rock, Mississippi

Tom Hodge . . . . .Houston, Mississippi

Charles Holder Vance . . . . .Gulfport, Mississippi

Darrel Vance . . . . .Gulfport, Mississipppi

Maurice Harris . . . . .Parker, Colorado

Robert Bates . . . . .Taylorsville, Mississippi

Kenneth Blakeny . . . . .Taylorsville, Mississippi

Jeannette Walker . . . . .Laurel, Mississippi

Helen Reeden . . . . .Laurel, Mississippi

Lex Lindsey . . . . .Laurel & Seattle

Lynn Lindsey . . . . .Laurel & Seattle

Ron Robinson . . . . .Bay Springs

Mary Robinson . . . . .Bay Springs

Eric Adams . . . . .Ovett, Mississippi

Evelyn Adams . . . . .Ovett, Mississippi

Eli Adams . . . . .Ovett, Mississippi

Brenda Brown . . . . .Magee, Mississippi

Jan Burmeister . . . . .Frankfort, Germany

Daniel Williams . . . . .Pass Christian, Mississippi

Mr. Vedding .Pass Christian, Mississippi

Dan Kinneson . . . . .Gulfport, Mississippi

Mattie B. Wilks . . . . .Coldwater, Mississippi

Barbara M. George . . . . .Memphis, Tennessee

Davey, this is a list of people I did not want as customers. Yet, they came every day or 3 or 4 times a week.

Steve Aycock
Deon Robinson
Mark Ishee
Randy Corley
Lee Upton
Keith Sims
Wesley Henry
Carter Sims (not Morgan Sims)
Lonnie Phillip
Jack Upton
Terry L. Simmons
Joe Jo Sims
Harvey Curry (Newton Police Chief)
Jeff Hopkins (my chicken & fish man)
Frankie McCullen, Newton Police
Chris Sims
Chris McDonald (Grandson)
Melvin Shipp (Grandson)
Valeria McCray
Julia Welborn
Kenneth Jones (Fire Truck)
Don Hurst
Todd Mathis (Salesman, Newell Paper Co.)
Ida Mosely
Rose Keller
H. B. Bender
Ronnie Buckley (Buckley Newspaper Pub.)
Thad (JC) Moncrief
Bruce Smiley
Craig Byrd
Brian (Newton Police)
The Peco Boys:
Ronnie Tolbert, Russ Burnette, Travis Sellers,
Red Scott (not Phil Scott),
Kip Simpson, Benny Sumrall, Tracy Boyd,
Billy Ray Sims, Ralph Smith
Walter Phillips

Warren King
Arnold (Frank) Buckley
Jammie Baccum
Stephen Rhodes
Al Kennedy
Erving Brown
Jay (J Bird) Phillip
Lance Garvin
Sharron Shipp (Daughter-in-law)
Ray Rayner
Kendey Blackeny
Mike McNeil
Bill May (Lawyer)
Robert Logan (Lawyer, "Tight-wad")
Rusty McMullum (Lawyer)
Mike Gieger (Banker)
Ted Herrington
Chuck Edwards
Mike Price
Steve Lindsey
Mike Campbell
Frankie Johnson (Hospital Administrator)
Joel Monk (my main meat cutter)
Ricky Horton & his son, Richard
Criss McDonald (grandson)
Mike Butler (Newton Piggly Wiggly)
Ronald (Wet Back) Roberts
Cliff Richardson (man from Garlandville)
Zack Buckley (Buckley Newspapers)
Shannon
Wesley Hall
Mr. & Mrs. Glenn Parker
Rose Harrington
Gina Thomas
Ron Peck
Karen Burns
Bodie Myrick
Dave C. Doby
Last but not least, Rev. Bro. John Earl Bowen, Jr.

If I missed anyone, I hate you too!

Davy, just a few notes from customers.
I think you might enjoy reading

Sister Earline:

The bible tells of how Jesus
Loved to fellowship
And also of how he liked to eat.
Truly, it's a great blessing from God.
If I never eat again,
I've had mine;
For I've dined at Davey's,
And the meal was divine.

God Be With You,

Frederick Handel Craft

My dear, dear Friend;

I am thinking about you and the Christmas season fast approaching. I hope your <u>Christmas time</u> and the <u>New Year</u> will be filled with the <u>presence</u>, <u>preeminence</u> and <u>peace of the Lord</u> - not only for you but for Davy and your other loved ones (including Chris and Melvin) and your host of friends many in number. May the blessings of good health cloth you for many days!

Your friend, **Marion**

15 July 2005

Dear Ms Broomfield,

We are grateful to the Bay Springs gentleman who told us to eat Sunday dinner at Miss Earline's place.

The food was delicious and you and your staff were so friendly that we felt right at home. As it turned out, escaping from Hurricane Dennis was a very pleasant adventure.

We look forward to our next visit to your restaurant and we are busy telling our friends to be sure to stop at Davey's for some of Miss Earline's fine cooking.

Sincerely,
Mr. & Mrs. Bernard Gautier

To: Mrs Earline **AND** the Davey's Restaurant Staff.

Thank you for being so kind to me during my visit. There are not many places where you can walk in and feel at home right away. I look forward to coming back to visit and winning my $40.00 back. Keep up the good work and I'll see you all soon.

Sheryl

Nov. 29, 2002

Miss Earline

The whole May family wishes you could have seen us eating the delicious food you cooked for us on Thanksgiving.

Everything you cooked was so good, and we enjoyed it all so much!

Thanks for making our Thanksgiving such a fun and fulfilling time.

Bill's Mom, **Chlori May**

Dear Mrs. Earline Broomfield,

Thank you so much for the autographed copy of your cookbook. My wife was so exited to see a twist on some of the recipes that she was already familiar with. She is anxious to try out about half your book. I know I'm looking forward to it already. Aside from the recipes I like the family history and photos you provide in your cookbook. It's a piece of living history. I hope your children appreciate what a wonderful mother they have in all that your do for your family, community, church and friends. I will be praying that your knee get's to feeling better and that you be bless in all that you do. I look forward to taking care of you at Dr. Brumley's office.

Always your friend, **John Sumner**

Dear Mrs. Earline,

Thanks you for your warm and gracious hospitality to us on early Friday morning.

Meeting and talking with you and your staff was such an honor. Of course, your homemade biscuits would have been a special "topping" too, but the short visit there (and the cake) was superb!! You represent Mississippi's best!

Sincerely,
Sara Dollar Thorpe

Thank you so very much! I enjoyed reading your cookbook (the one my grandson, Nic Norton recently bought for his mom. She will love it!). Hog killing and canning of the meat brought back so many memories. Your book is a treasure. God bless you.

June Norton; 201 Mt Salus; Clinton, MS 390561

Whose Job Is It?

This is story about four people named Everybody, Somebody, Anybody and Nobody. There was an important job to be done and Everybody was asked to do it. Everybody was sure Somebody would do it. Anybody could have done it, but Nobody did it.

Somebody got angry about that, because it was Everybody's job. Everybody thought Anybody could do it, but Nobody realized that Everybody wouldn't do it.

It ended up that Everybody blamed Somebody when Nobody did what Anybody could have done.

(copied)

Donated by **Rose Keller,**
a special friend

THE WHITE HOUSE

July 22, 2005

Mrs. Earline Edison Broomfield
5628 Highway 15
Louin, Mississippi 39338-4219

Dear Mrs. Broomfield,

Thank you for sending an inscribed copy of Volume 2 of *Davey's Restaurant Country Cooking.* Your recipes sound like great southern treasures.

I hope I can visit your restaurant someday.

With best wishes,

Laura Bush

Davey, these old sayings were handed down from your great grandma and your grandmother.

1. Get shed of--Throw Out
2. Cooking Vessels--Pots and pans
3. If I had my druthers--If I had my way
4. Not worth a hill of beans--Not worth much
5. To reckley-- In a little while
6. Mite near--Almost
7. Near about--Almost
8. Make ace--Hurry
9. Hold your taters--Wait
10. Some how or nuther--Some way
11. Putting on the dog--Trying to impress
12. Bed stid--Head board
13. Tied up--Busy
14. Spring chicken--Young person
15. Stove up--Soreness of muscles
16. On a low lim--Down on your luck
17. Stands ot reason--Make sense
18. To pooped to pop--Tired
19. Not enough to say grace over--Very little food
20. Gal I cus--Suspenders
21. Lassese--Syrup or molesses
22. Gallerie--Porch
23. Step-ins--Ladies panties
24. Directly--Soon
25. 2 Bits --is fifty cents
26. 4 Bits--is 1 dollar
27. Juke joint--A southern night club
28. Goobers--Peanuts
29. Whole hay or none--The best or nothing
30. Haint-Ghost
31. Dry up--Be quiet
32. Tote--Carry
33. Every dog will have its day--You will reap what you sow
34. Rooster bullets--Eggs

35. High hill crime--Real good time
36. Parlor--Living room
37. From the git go--From the beginning
38. Fall Off--Lose weight
39. Heading for the hay--Going to bed

Goodnight, Davey Doby, Glenn Parker, Christopher McDonald, and Melvin (Poochie) Skipp.

Goodnight, John Boy! (Smile)

NOTES

_____

_____

_____

_____

_____

_____

_____

_____

_____

_____

_____

_____

_____

_____

_____

_____

_____

_____

NOTES

NOTES